Mastering Microsoft Power Apps

A Comprehensive Step-by-Step Guide for Beginners

By
James Flux

<u>Disclaimer</u>

The information in this book is provided for educational purposes only. While every effort has been made to ensure the accuracy and completeness of the content, the author and publisher make no representations or warranties regarding the accuracy, reliability, or suitability of the information for any particular purpose. The reader is advised to use their own judgment and discretion when applying any of the techniques or recommendations mentioned in this book.

Dedication

To all the learners and creators, who are ready to embrace the future with curiosity and passion.

This book is for you—may it guide you on your journey from beginner to pro in the world of Power Apps.

May each page inspire you to build, innovate, and unlock new possibilities for your success.

Microsoft Power Apps

Contents

Introduction

Technology is constantly evolving, and businesses are looking for faster, more efficient ways to build applications without relying on complex coding. Microsoft Power Apps has transformed the way organizations create custom solutions, enabling users to design apps that improve workflows, automate tasks, and enhance productivity – all with little to no coding experience.

This book is your **comprehensive guide** to understanding and mastering Power Apps. Whether you're a beginner taking your first steps into low-code development or an experienced professional looking to expand your knowledge, this book will equip you with the skills to **build powerful business applications effortlessly**.

Updates to Power Apps

Microsoft continuously enhances Power Apps by adding **new features, integrations, and AI-driven capabilities**. Recent updates have made app development even more seamless, including:

- **Improved AI-powered automation** – With AI Builder and Power Automate, you can create smarter workflows and datadriven applications.
- **Enhanced user interface components** – New templates, controls, and design elements allow for more intuitive and visually appealing apps.
- **Better integration with Microsoft Teams** – You can now embed Power Apps directly into Teams, improving team collaboration

and workflow automation.

- **Advanced security and governance** – More control over permissions, data security, and compliance measures ensures that apps remain safe and scalable.

These updates empower users to build more sophisticated applications with minimal effort, helping businesses **save time, reduce costs, and improve efficiency**.

Who This Book Is For

This book is designed for a wide range of readers, including:

- **Beginners** who want to build business apps without needing deep technical skills.
- **Business professionals** looking to automate processes and enhance productivity.
- **IT and software developers** interested in leveraging Power Apps for rapid application development.
- **Entrepreneurs and startups** aiming to create cost-effective solutions tailored to their needs.

No matter your background, if you want to **transform ideas into functional applications** without the complexities of traditional coding, this book will guide you every step of the way.

What This Book Covers

This book provides a structured, **step-by-step approach** to mastering Power Apps. You will learn how to:

- **Understand the fundamentals** of Power Apps and low-code development.

- **Design user-friendly applications** with intuitive interfaces.
- **Integrate Power Apps** with Microsoft Teams, SharePoint, and third-party services.
- **Leverage AI and automation** to enhance business operations.
- **Test, debug, and optimize** apps for different devices and platforms.
- **Publish, share, and distribute** apps within organizations.
- **Manage security, permissions, and governance** for enterpriselevel applications.

By the end of this book, you will have the knowledge and confidence to **build, manage, and deploy business applications** that drive real impact.

How to Get the Most Out of This Book

To ensure you **maximize your learning experience**, follow these recommendations:

1. **Follow Along with Hands-On Exercises** – This book includes practical examples and exercises to help you apply concepts in real-world scenarios.
2. **Experiment and Explore** – Don't just read—practice by building sample apps and testing different features.
3. **Utilize Online Resources** – Microsoft provides extensive documentation and a strong community to help you when you need additional guidance.
4. **Stay Updated with Power Apps Enhancements** – As Power Apps evolves, keep learning and exploring new features to improve your applications.

With the right mindset and a willingness to explore, you will soon become proficient in **building no-code and low-code applications** that transform how businesses operate.

Let's begin your journey to mastering **Microsoft Power Apps!**

Chapter 1: Introduction to Power Apps

1.1 What is Microsoft Power Apps?

Technology is constantly evolving, and businesses need tools that can keep up with the rapid changes. Microsoft Power Apps is one such tool—designed to help individuals and organizations create powerful, custom applications without requiring extensive coding knowledge. It enables users to build apps that automate tasks, improve efficiency, and enhance productivity, all while integrating seamlessly with Microsoft's ecosystem and other data sources.

At its core, Power Apps is a low-code application development platform that allows anyone, from beginners to professionals, to create apps that solve real-world problems. Whether you are a business owner looking to streamline operations, an employee trying to improve workflow, or a developer seeking a more efficient way to build applications, Power Apps provides the flexibility and tools needed to bring ideas to life.

Breaking Down the Concept

Power Apps simplifies the app development process by offering a visual interface where users can drag and drop elements, connect to various data sources, and add logic without writing complex code. This makes it accessible to individuals who may not have a background in programming but still want to create functional and visually appealing applications.

With Power Apps, you can:

- Design **custom applications** tailored to specific business needs
- Connect with multiple **data sources**, such as SharePoint, Excel, and Microsoft Dataverse
- Automate **manual processes** to save time and effort
- Build **responsive apps** that work seamlessly on desktops, tablets, and mobile devices
- **Integrate AI-powered features** to enhance user experience

Why is Power Apps Important?

Businesses today rely on technology to operate efficiently, and Power Apps bridges the gap between the need for automation and the complexity of traditional app development. Before Power Apps, creating a business application required hiring professional developers, investing significant time and money, and navigating complex coding frameworks. Now, with a simplified approach, organizations can quickly develop solutions without the high costs and lengthy development timelines.

Even for individuals, Power Apps provides a way to build personal productivity tools, automate repetitive tasks, and improve efficiency without needing advanced technical skills.

Types of Power Apps

Microsoft Power Apps is divided into three main categories, each designed for different use cases:

1. Canvas Apps

These apps start with a blank canvas, allowing users to design their interface from scratch by dragging and dropping components like buttons, text fields, and images. This type of app provides the most creative freedom, as you can structure it exactly the way you want.

Example Use Cases:

- A **customized expense tracking app** for employees
- A **customer feedback form** that integrates with a database
- An **inventory management system** tailored to business needs

2. Model-Driven Apps

Unlike canvas apps, model-driven apps follow a data-first approach, meaning the structure and user interface are automatically generated based on the data model. This is ideal for complex applications that require detailed data management and business process automation.

Example Use Cases:

- A **customer relationship management (CRM) system**
- A **project tracking tool** for managing deadlines and tasks
- A **case management system** for support teams

3. Portal Apps

These are web-based apps that allow external users, such as customers or partners, to interact with business data securely. They are commonly used for self-service portals, customer support systems, and community engagement platforms.

Example Use Cases:

- A **self-service portal for customers to check order status**
- A **job application platform for HR departments**
- A **membership site for exclusive content and resources**

How Power Apps Transforms Workflows

Before Power Apps, businesses relied on spreadsheets, emails, and manual processes to manage their operations. This often led to inefficiencies, data inconsistencies, and a lack of real-time insights. By introducing Power Apps into your workflow, you can automate these processes, ensuring better accuracy, speed, and collaboration.

For example, imagine a company that tracks employee attendance using paper-based forms. Employees fill out forms manually, HR personnel collect them, input the data into a spreadsheet, and generate reports. This process is time-consuming and prone to errors.

With Power Apps, this company can build a **custom attendance tracking app** where employees log their attendance digitally, and the data is automatically stored, processed, and analyzed. HR can then generate real-time reports with a single click, saving time and improving accuracy.

Key Features That Make Power Apps Stand Out

- **Drag-and-Drop Interface** – No need to write complex code; simply select components and arrange them on the screen.
- **AI Builder** – Integrate AI-powered features like text recognition, prediction models, and chatbots into your apps.
- **Seamless Integration** – Connect with Microsoft 365, SharePoint, Dynamics 365, Azure, and third-party applications.

- **Cross-Platform Support** – Build apps that work on desktops, tablets, and mobile devices without additional coding.
- **Security and Compliance** – Ensure data security with rolebased access and Microsoft's enterprise-grade security standards.

Getting Started with Power Apps

Now that you understand what Power Apps is and why it's beneficial, let's walk through the basic steps to start using it:

Step 1: Sign in to Power Apps

1. Go to the Power Apps website (or open the Power Apps desktop app).
2. Sign in using your **Microsoft 365 account**. If you don't have one, you can create a free trial account.

Step 2: Choose the Type of App You Want to Build

- Select **Canvas App** if you want complete design freedom.
- Choose **Model-Driven App** if you need a structured, data-first application.
- Pick **Portal App** if you need an external-facing web app.

Step 3: Select a Data Source

- Click on **Data** in the left panel and connect to sources like SharePoint, Excel, or Microsoft Dataverse.
- If needed, create a new **table or database** for storing your app's information.

Step 4: Design the User Interface

- Drag and drop elements like text boxes, buttons, and images onto the canvas.
- Customize fonts, colors, and layout to match your branding.
- Add navigation screens and input fields as needed.

Step 5: Add Logic and Automation

- Use **Power Fx**, a simple formula-based language, to define actions and conditions.
- Set up **buttons** to trigger workflows, such as sending emails or updating records.
- Integrate **Power Automate** for advanced automation.

Step 6: Test and Publish Your App

- Click **Preview** to see how your app works in real time.
- Make adjustments if necessary, ensuring everything functions as expected.
- Once satisfied, **publish and share** the app with your team or organization.

1.2 Overview of Power Apps Ecosystem

Technology is no longer reserved for software developers and IT specialists. With Microsoft Power Apps, anyone—whether an entrepreneur, a business professional, or a team leader—can build applications that simplify tasks, automate workflows, and enhance productivity. However, to fully harness its potential, it is essential to understand the broader ecosystem that supports it.

Power Apps is not a standalone tool; it is part of a dynamic environment that integrates seamlessly with various Microsoft services and external platforms. This ecosystem provides users with the necessary tools to create, connect, and deploy applications that serve real-world needs.

The Key Components of the Power Apps Ecosystem

Microsoft has designed Power Apps to work in harmony with other services, making app development faster and more efficient. The ecosystem consists of several crucial elements, each playing a specific role in creating powerful, user-friendly applications.

1. Power Apps Studio – The Heart of App Development

Power Apps Studio is where applications come to life. It provides an intuitive, drag-and-drop interface where users can design layouts, add features, and build applications without writing extensive code.

How to Access Power Apps Studio:

1. Sign in to **Power Apps** using your Microsoft account.
2. Click on **Create an App** and choose from **Canvas App, Model Driven App, or Portal App** based on your needs.
3. Start designing your app by adding text fields, buttons, images, and other components.

Power Apps Studio allows complete control over the look and feel of an application. Users can customize layouts, set navigation paths, and connect to data sources—all from a single interface.

2. Power Apps Admin Center – Managing and Monitoring Apps

The **Power Apps Admin Center** is a management hub where users can oversee apps, monitor performance, and enforce security policies. It provides a clear view of all applications running in an organization, helping administrators maintain control over data access and user permissions.

Key Features of Power Apps Admin Center:

- **App Management:** View and manage all applications created within the organization.
- **Security & Compliance:** Set permissions, manage data policies, and ensure compliance with organizational standards.
- **Performance Monitoring:** Track app performance and resolve any issues in real time.

3. Microsoft Dataverse – The Central Data Hub

Data is the foundation of any application. Microsoft Dataverse (formerly known as Common Data Service) acts as a structured database where all app-related data can be stored, retrieved, and managed efficiently.

How Microsoft Dataverse Enhances Power Apps:

- **Centralized Data Storage:** Keep all information in a single location for easy access and organization.
- **Security Controls:** Define who can access or edit data, ensuring privacy and protection.
- **Integration with Other Microsoft Services:** Automatically syncs with Dynamics 365, SharePoint, and other Microsoft tools.

For businesses that deal with large amounts of data, Dataverse simplifies data management, making it easier to build powerful applications without worrying about backend storage complexities.

4. Connectors – Bridging Power Apps with Other Services

One of the most powerful aspects of Power Apps is its ability to connect with different data sources. **Connectors** serve as bridges that link Power Apps to external platforms, allowing seamless data exchange.

Types of Connectors in Power Apps:

- **Standard Connectors** – Pre-built connections to common services like Microsoft 365, OneDrive, and Outlook.
- **Premium Connectors** – Advanced integrations with external systems such as Salesforce, SQL Server, and SAP.
- **Custom Connectors** – Users can build their own connectors to link Power Apps with unique third-party applications.

For example, a company can create an **employee expense tracking app** that pulls data from **Excel, integrates approvals through Outlook, and stores receipts in SharePoint**, all using connectors.

5. Power Automate – Automating Workflows with Intelligence

Power Automate works alongside Power Apps to streamline repetitive tasks. It enables users to set up automated workflows that trigger specific actions when certain conditions are met.

Examples of Power Automate in Action:

- **Auto-approval workflows:** When an employee submits a leave request in Power Apps, Power Automate can send it for approval automatically.

- **Instant notifications:** A sales tracking app can notify managers when an order is placed.
- **Data updates:** Sync customer information from an app to a database without manual input.

This integration ensures that apps remain efficient, reducing manual effort while increasing productivity.

6. AI Builder – Enhancing Apps with Artificial Intelligence

Microsoft Power Apps includes **AI Builder**, a tool that allows users to integrate artificial intelligence into applications without needing a background in machine learning.

How AI Builder Adds Intelligence to Apps:

- **Text Recognition:** Automatically extracts information from invoices, receipts, and handwritten documents.
- **Prediction Models:** Helps businesses forecast trends based on historical data.
- **Chatbots:** Enhances customer service by allowing apps to respond to user queries using AI-driven bots.

By using AI Builder, businesses can create smarter applications that analyze data, recognize patterns, and automate decision-making processes.

/. Power BI – Bringing Data to Life with Visualization

Data without insights is just numbers. Power BI is a data visualization tool that works with Power Apps to transform raw data into interactive reports and dashboards.

How Power BI Works with Power Apps:

- **Real-time Analytics:** Track business performance through visual reports.
- **Interactive Dashboards:** Allow users to filter and explore data within Power Apps.
- **Seamless Integration:** Embed Power BI reports directly into Power Apps for better decision-making.

For instance, a **sales tracking app** can include a Power BI dashboard that visually represents **monthly sales, customer demographics, and revenue growth**, helping businesses make informed choices.

How the Power Apps Ecosystem Works Together

All these components are interconnected, creating a seamless experience for users. Power Apps acts as the **application builder**, Microsoft Dataverse serves as the **data storage**, Connectors allow integration with **external services**, and Power Automate brings in **automation**. Meanwhile, **AI Builder** and **Power BI** enhance intelligence and visualization capabilities.

For example, a **customer service app** built using Power Apps can:

1. **Store customer complaints** in Dataverse.
2. **Automatically assign cases** using Power Automate.
3. **Analyze complaint trends** with Power BI.

4. **Use AI Builder** to extract details from complaint forms.

This interconnected system ensures efficiency, reduces manual work, and provides businesses with smarter tools to operate effectively.

1.3 Key Features of Power Apps

Microsoft Power Apps is designed to make app development simple, efficient, and accessible to everyone. Whether you are a business professional, a team leader, or an entrepreneur, Power Apps provides the tools needed to create functional applications without requiring deep coding knowledge. But what makes Power Apps truly powerful? It is the combination of features that enable users to design, automate, and integrate applications seamlessly.

Understanding these key features will give you a solid foundation for building apps that solve real-world problems, improve productivity, and enhance user experience.

1. No-Code/Low-Code Development – Build Apps with Ease

Gone are the days when creating an application required writing thousands of lines of complex code. Power Apps follows a **no-code/lowcode** approach, allowing users to **drag and drop components**, set up workflows, and integrate data without programming expertise.

How to Build an App Without Coding:

1. **Open Power Apps Studio** – Start by accessing the intuitive design interface.
2. **Choose a Template or Start from Scratch** – Pick a pre-built template for faster development or create a custom app.
3. **Drag and Drop Elements** – Add text fields, buttons, images, and forms to structure your application.
4. **Set Up Rules and Actions** – Define how the app should respond to user input using simple logic settings.
5. **Preview and Publish** – Test the app in real time and make it available for use within your organization.

This feature empowers people from all backgrounds to create applications tailored to their specific needs without spending months in development.

2. Seamless Integration with Microsoft 365 and Other Services

Power Apps does not work in isolation; it connects effortlessly with various Microsoft tools such as **Excel, SharePoint, Outlook, and Teams**. This integration ensures that data flows smoothly between applications, eliminating the need for manual data entry.

Examples of How Integration Enhances Workflows:

- **HR teams** can create an app that tracks employee leave requests and syncs them with Outlook calendars.
- **Sales teams** can build a customer management system that updates records directly in Excel.

- **Project managers** can design a task-tracking app that links to SharePoint for real-time collaboration.

Beyond Microsoft services, Power Apps also integrates with external platforms like Salesforce, Dropbox, and Twitter, making it a flexible tool for any organization.

3. Multiple App Types for Different Needs

Power Apps offers three primary types of applications, each designed for specific use cases.

A. Canvas Apps – Full Control Over Design

Canvas apps give users complete freedom to design applications from a blank canvas. You can customize every detail, add different elements, and control the user experience entirely.

Example: A company can create a **field service app** where technicians enter service details on-site using a mobile-friendly interface.

B. Model-Driven Apps – Data-Powered Applications

Model-driven apps focus on data-driven processes. Instead of designing an app from scratch, you start by defining the data structure, and Power Apps automatically generates the layout.

Example: A **customer support ticketing system** can be built using model-driven apps, where each ticket follows a structured workflow.

C. Portal Apps – External User Access

Portal apps allow organizations to build web-based applications that external users (such as customers or vendors) can access securely.
   Example: A company can create a **customer self-service portal** where users submit requests and track updates.

4. Pre-Built Templates for Faster Development

Not everyone wants to build an app from the ground up. Power Apps provides **pre-built templates** that cater to common business needs, allowing users to get started quickly.

How to Use a Template:

1. **Open Power Apps and Navigate to Templates**
2. **Browse Different Categories** – Choose from HR, finance, sales, project management, and other templates.
3. **Customize the Template** – Modify the fields, colors, and workflows to match your requirements.
4. **Test and Deploy** – Once the changes are made, preview and publish the app for immediate use.

Using templates saves time and ensures best practices in app design.

5. Built-In AI Capabilities for Smarter Apps

Power Apps includes **AI Builder**, an artificial intelligence tool that enhances applications by adding intelligence-driven features. This means users can incorporate AI into their apps **without needing advanced technical knowledge**.

What AI Can Do in Power Apps:

- **Recognize Text and Handwriting:** Extract information from invoices, receipts, or scanned documents.
- **Analyze Sentiment:** Determine customer satisfaction based on feedback in surveys or social media posts.
- **Detect Objects in Images:** Identify products in stock or detect items for quality control in a manufacturing setting.

This feature enables businesses to make data-driven decisions and automate complex processes with minimal effort.

6. Cross-Platform Compatibility – Access Apps Anywhere

One of the biggest advantages of Power Apps is that applications are **compatible across multiple devices**. Whether users are on a **desktop, tablet, or smartphone**, they can access and interact with applications without issues.

How Cross-Platform Compatibility Benefits Users:

- Employees working in the field can **update data from their mobile devices**.
- Managers can **approve requests on tablets** without needing to log into a computer.
- Remote teams can **collaborate seamlessly** using cloud-based access.

Power Apps ensures that users are not restricted to a single platform, increasing flexibility and efficiency.

7. Secure and Scalable for Business Growth

Security is a critical aspect of any application, and Power Apps ensures **enterprise-level protection**. Organizations can define **role-based access controls**, meaning only authorized users can view or modify data.

Security Features in Power Apps:

- **Data encryption** – Protects sensitive information from unauthorized access.
- **Role-based permissions** – Limits user actions based on job roles.
- **Multi-factor authentication** – Adds an extra layer of security for login verification.

Additionally, Power Apps is scalable, meaning businesses can start with simple applications and expand functionality as their needs grow.

8. Automation with Power Automate – Streamlining Workflows

Power Apps works hand in hand with **Power Automate**, allowing users to set up automated workflows that save time and reduce errors.

Examples of Automated Processes:

- **Send an approval request** when an employee submits an expense report.
- **Trigger an email notification** when a new lead is added to the system.
- **Move data between apps** without requiring manual updates.

2

By integrating automation, organizations can eliminate repetitive tasks and focus on more strategic work.

1.4 Types of Power Apps: Canvas Apps vs. Model-Driven Apps

Power Apps is designed to provide flexibility in application development, ensuring that businesses and individuals can create solutions tailored to their needs. It offers two main types of applications: **Canvas Apps** and **Model-Driven Apps**. Each type serves a distinct purpose and is suited for different scenarios. Understanding their differences will help you choose the right approach for your app development journey.

Canvas Apps – Full Control Over Design and Layout

Canvas Apps give you complete freedom to design your application from scratch. You start with a **blank canvas** and build the app by adding elements such as buttons, text fields, images, and forms. This approach is ideal for those who want to create a highly customized user experience with complete control over layout and design.

Key Features of Canvas Apps:

- Full **drag-and-drop** customization
- **No strict data structure** – you define how data is displayed and stored

- **Flexible UI design** – you control every element's placement and behavior
- Ideal for mobile and tablet-friendly applications

When to Use Canvas Apps?

Canvas Apps work best when you need a **highly customized user interface** and want to control every detail of how users interact with the app.

How to Create a Canvas App?

1. **Open Power Apps Studio** – This is the main development environment for creating apps.
2. **Choose "Canvas App"** – Select whether you want the app for a phone or tablet.
3. **Select a Data Source** – Connect to sources like Excel, SharePoint, or SQL databases.
4. **Design the Layout** – Drag and drop buttons, text fields, images, and other elements.
5. **Set Up User Actions** – Define how the app should respond to user input.
6. **Test and Publish** – Once satisfied, preview and deploy the app for users.

Canvas Apps are perfect for **field service apps, employee portals, customer request forms, and inventory tracking tools**, where flexibility in layout is a priority.

Model-Driven Apps – Structured, Data-Focused Applications

Unlike Canvas Apps, Model-Driven Apps are based on **predefined data models**. The layout and user interface are automatically generated based on the data structure, making it an excellent choice for applications that need to follow specific business rules and processes.

Key Features of Model-Driven Apps:

- **Data-driven design** – The structure is based on the Microsoft Dataverse
- **Pre-built UI elements** – Forms, dashboards, and views are autogenerated
- **Ideal for complex business processes**
- **Built-in security and role management**

When to Use Model-Driven Apps?

Model-Driven Apps are best suited for scenarios where the app needs to follow structured workflows and handle large amounts of data in an organized way.

How to Create a Model-Driven App?

1. **Go to Power Apps and Select "Model-Driven App"**
2. **Define the Data Model** – Use Microsoft Dataverse to set up tables and relationships.
3. **Customize Forms and Views** – Modify how data is displayed and interacted with.
4. **Set Up Business Logic** – Automate processes using workflows

and rules.

5. **Test the App** – Check its functionality before deployment.
6. **Publish and Share** – Make the app available to users within your organization.

Model-Driven Apps are commonly used for **customer service management, sales tracking, employee onboarding systems, and case management applications**—where structured workflows are necessary.

Canvas Apps vs. Model-Driven Apps – Which One Should You Choose?

Feature	Canvas Apps	Model-Driven Apps
Design Control	Full customization	Auto-generated UI
Data Structure	Flexible, connects to various sources	Strictly based on Microsoft Dataverse
Ideal For	Mobile-first apps, custom UI, forms, and dashboards	Business process automation, structured workflows
Development Approach	Drag-and-drop, manual layout setup	Data-driven, predefined structure
Best Use Cases	Inventory tracking, field service apps, customer request forms	Sales tracking, HR management, case management systems

Choosing the right type depends on your business requirements. If you want total creative control over design, **Canvas Apps** is the way to go. If your focus is on structured business processes and data management, **Model-Driven Apps** is the better choice.

1.5 Power Apps Licensing Models

Understanding Power Apps licensing is crucial before diving into app development. Microsoft offers different licensing models to ensure flexibility for businesses and individuals. Whether you need Power Apps for a single project, multiple users, or development purposes, there's a plan suited to your needs. In this section, we will explore the three main licensing models: **Per-User Plan, Per-App Plan, and Developer Plan.**

1.5.1 Per-User Plan – Full Access for Individuals

The **Per-User Plan** is designed for individuals who need full access to create and run multiple apps without restrictions. This plan is best suited for employees, developers, and business users who actively build and manage apps within an organization.

Key Features of the Per-User Plan:

- Allows **unlimited app creation and usage** within an organization
- Includes access to **Microsoft Dataverse,** the structured data storage system
- Supports **premium connectors,** which enable integration with advanced data sources
- Provides automation capabilities through **Power Automate**

Who Should Choose the Per-User Plan?

This plan is ideal for professionals who require **full control over app development** without being limited by the number of apps they can build or use.

How to Get Started with the Per-User Plan?

1. **Sign in to the Power Apps Portal** – Use your Microsoft account.
2. **Go to the Licensing Section** – Navigate to the "Plans & Pricing" tab.
3. **Select the Per-User Plan** – Choose the option that fits your needs.
4. **Complete the Purchase** – Enter payment details or assign the plan to your organization.
5. **Start Building Apps** – Once activated, you can develop unlimited applications.

The Per-User Plan is a **cost-effective choice for businesses** that need multiple apps and want to provide employees with unrestricted access to Power Apps.

1.5.2 Per-App Plan – Pay for What You Use

The **Per-App Plan** is designed for organizations that only need specific applications rather than full access to unlimited app development. Instead of paying for each user, you **only pay for the specific apps** used within your organization.

Key Features of the Per-App Plan:

- Grants access to **one or two specific apps** per user
- Supports **premium connectors** and **Dataverse integration**
- Includes **basic automation features** via Power Automate
- More affordable for companies that don't need unlimited apps

Who Should Choose the Per-App Plan?

This plan is best for businesses that want **limited access to Power Apps** for certain teams or departments. If your company only needs one or two apps for operations, this plan helps **reduce costs** while maintaining efficiency.

How to Get Started with the Per-App Plan?

1. **Visit the Power Apps Pricing Page** – Access it through your Microsoft account.
2. **Select the Per-App Plan** – Choose the number of apps you need.
3. **Assign Users to the Apps** – Decide which employees or teams will have access.
4. **Confirm and Purchase** – Finalize the subscription and activate the license.
5. **Deploy and Manage the App** – Users can now access the app(s) under this plan.

The **Per-App Plan is perfect for businesses with focused needs**, such as customer service management, inventory tracking, or employee portals, without requiring access to multiple applications.

1.5.3 Developer Plan – Build and Test Apps for Free

The **Developer Plan** is an excellent option for **developers, learners, and testers** who want to explore Power Apps without paying for a full license. This plan allows users to **build and test applications** in a sandbox environment without affecting live production data.

Key Features of the Developer Plan:

- **Completely free** – No cost for development and testing
- Includes **Microsoft Dataverse** for structured data management
- Provides access to **premium connectors** for integration testing
- Cannot be used for **business or commercial production apps**

Who Should Choose the Developer Plan?

This plan is **ideal for students, developers, and IT professionals** who want to **practice app development** before deploying them in a live business setting. It's also great for those **experimenting with Power Apps' features** before committing to a paid plan.

How to Get Started with the Developer Plan?

1. **Go to the Power Apps Developer Plan Page** – Log in with your Microsoft account.
2. **Sign Up for Free** – No credit card or payment is required.
3. **Set Up Your Developer Environment** – A sandbox is created for you.
4. **Start Building and Testing** – Use premium connectors and Dataverse without restrictions.
5. **Upgrade When Ready** – If you want to deploy apps commercially

update to a paid plan.

The **Developer Plan is an excellent starting point** for those who want to **learn Power Apps, build prototypes, and test integrations** without financial commitment.

Choosing the Right Licensing Model

Licensing Model	Best For	Key Benefit	Cost
Per-User Plan	Individuals who need unlimited access	Full control over app development	Paid
Per-App Plan	Organizations needing only a few apps	Cost-effective for specific business needs	Paid (Per App)
Developer Plan	Developers, learners, and testers	Free access for testing and learning	Free

Chapter 2: Navigating the Power Apps Studio

2.1 Introduction to Power Apps Studio Interface

Microsoft Power Apps Studio is the foundation where ideas take shape, transforming concepts into fully functional applications. Whether you are a beginner or an experienced developer, understanding the Power Apps Studio interface is essential for building, customizing, and managing applications efficiently.

Power Apps Studio provides a user-friendly, visual environment where you can create applications without needing extensive coding skills. The platform is designed to be **intuitive and interactive**, allowing you to **drag and drop elements, configure app settings, and integrate data sources seamlessly**.

Understanding the Layout of Power Apps Studio

When you launch Power Apps Studio, you are greeted with a well-organized workspace. The interface is divided into several key sections, each serving a distinct purpose. Familiarizing yourself with these sections will help you **navigate smoothly and maximize efficiency**.

1. The App Canvas – Your Design Space

At the heart of Power Apps Studio lies the **App Canvas**, the space where you design and build your application. Think of it as your **drawing board**, where you can **add buttons, images, forms, and other interactive elements**.

- **This is where you create the user interface**—the part of the app that your users will interact with.
- You can place components by **dragging and dropping** them onto the canvas.
- Each component can be **customized**, resized, and positioned to create a structured, visually appealing layout.

2. The Ribbon – Your Control Center

Located at the top of the screen, the **Ribbon** provides a collection of essential tools. It helps you **modify app elements, format text, and apply styles** without diving into complex settings.

- Contains **options for inserting components** like labels, buttons, and forms.
- Includes formatting tools for **adjusting colors, font styles, and**

alignment.

- Provides quick access to preview, save, and publish your app.

3. The Tree View – Organizing Your App's Structure

On the left side of the interface, you'll find the **Tree View**—a panel that displays all the components of your app in a structured manner.

- Lists every **screen, control, and data connection** used in your app.
- Helps you **organize and navigate** between different app sections efficiently.
- Makes it easier to **modify specific components** without searching through the entire app.

4. The Properties Panel – Customizing Components

On the right-hand side, the **Properties Panel** allows you to fine-tune the details of each component you add to your app. This panel changes dynamically based on what element you select.

- Modify properties such as **color, size, text, visibility, and behavior**.
- Adjust control settings to **customize the functionality** of buttons, text fields, and forms.
- Set up **data connections** to integrate your app with databases and other services.

5. The Formula Bar – Powering Your App with Logic

Directly above the App Canvas, you'll find the **Formula Bar**, which allows you to add logic to your application.

- Similar to formulas in **Excel**, this feature helps automate actions and control how elements behave.
- Used to create **dynamic responses**, such as making a button change color when clicked.
- Allows you to work with **data functions**, calculations, and conditions.

Step-by-Step Guide to Navigating Power Apps Studio

Now that you're familiar with the main sections of the interface, let's walk through a simple process to help you get started in Power Apps Studio.

Step 1: Open Power Apps Studio

- Sign in to **Power Apps** using your Microsoft account.
- On the home screen, select **Create an app** and choose either a **Canvas App** or a **Model-Driven App** (we will explore these types in a later section).
- Click on **Start from Blank** or choose a **pre-built template** to speed up development.

Step 2: Explore the App Canvas

- You will see an **empty design area** where you can start adding elements.
- Click on **Insert** in the Ribbon to add controls such as **buttons, text fields, or images**.
- Drag elements onto the canvas and arrange them to create the desired layout.

Step 3: Customize Components Using the Properties Panel

- Select any element on the canvas and open the **Properties Panel**.
- Modify settings like **color, font, alignment, and visibility**.
- Use the **Advanced Tab** for deeper customization and conditional formatting.

Step 4: Add Logic Using the Formula Bar

- Click on a button or text field and type a **formula** in the Formula Bar.
- For example, if you want a button to navigate to another screen when clicked, type:

```
Navigate(Screen2, ScreenTransition.Fade)
```

- This simple formula makes the app **move to Screen2 with a fade effect** when the button is pressed.

Step 5: Preview Your App

- Click the **Play Button** at the top-right corner of the screen to see how your app works in real time.
- Interact with the app, test buttons, and ensure everything functions as expected.

Step 6: Save and Publish Your App

- Click on **File > Save As** and name your app.
- Select **Publish** to make the app accessible to your team or organization.

Why Understanding the Interface Matters

Learning the Power Apps Studio interface is the **first step toward becoming proficient in app development**. A well-organized and structured workspace ensures:

- **Faster app creation** by using an intuitive drag-and-drop design.
- **Better control over customization** to match specific business or personal needs.
- **Seamless integration with data sources** for dynamic and functional applications.

2.2 Understanding Power Apps Components

To build a powerful, interactive, and user-friendly app in **Power Apps**, you need to understand its essential components. These components serve as the building blocks that bring your application to life, allowing users to **interact with data, navigate through screens, and perform tasks seamlessly**.

2.2.1 Controls, Forms, and Views

Controls – Adding Functionality to Your App

Controls are the **interactive elements** that allow users to **input information, trigger actions, and navigate** through an app. They play a crucial role in defining how users engage with the application.

Common Types of Controls

1. **Labels** – Display static text, such as titles, descriptions, or instructions.
2. **Text Inputs** – Allow users to enter information, such as names, emails, or numbers.
3. **Buttons** – Trigger specific actions, like submitting a form, navigating to another screen, or refreshing data.
4. **Dropdowns and Lists** – Provide selectable options for users to choose from.
5. **Galleries** – Display a list of items, such as a collection of products, contacts, or tasks.
6. **Toggle Switches and Checkboxes** – Allow users to enable or disable certain options.
7. **Media Controls** – Include images, videos, and audio for an

enhanced user experience.

How to Add and Use Controls

1. **Open Power Apps Studio** and navigate to the screen where you want to add a control.
2. Click on the **Insert** tab in the Ribbon at the top of the screen.
3. Select the desired **control type** (e.g., Button, Label, Text Input).
4. Drag the control onto the **App Canvas** and position it where needed.
5. Customize its properties using the **Properties Panel** on the right side.
6. Use the **Formula Bar** to add logic, such as:

```
If(TextInput1.Text = "Admin", Navigate(Screen2,
ScreenTransition.Fade))
```

1. This example allows users to navigate to another screen only if they enter "Admin" in the text box.

Forms – Capturing and Displaying Data

Forms are essential when your app needs to **collect user input or display structured data from a source**. They connect to databases, SharePoint lists, or Excel files, making them an integral part of data driven applications.

Types of Forms

1. **Edit Forms** – Allow users to enter or modify data.

2. **Display Forms** – Show existing data without allowing edits.

How to Use Forms in Your App

1. Click **Insert** > **Forms** in Power Apps Studio.
2. Choose **Edit Form** or **Display Form**, depending on your needs.
3. Connect the form to a **data source** by selecting one in the **Properties Panel**.
4. Add fields and configure them for **text, numbers, or dropdown selections**.
5. Use a **Submit Button** to save changes or send data to the database.

Views – Presenting Data in a Structured Way

Views define how **information is displayed in an app**, making it easier for users to find, filter, and interact with data.

Examples of Views

1. **List View** – Shows records in a structured format, such as a customer list.
2. **Detail View** – Displays detailed information about a single record.
3. **Gallery View** – Presents data in a visually rich format with images and descriptions.

How to Use Views in Power Apps

1. Insert a **Gallery Control** from the **Insert Tab**.
2. Connect it to a **data source**, such as a SharePoint list or SQL database.

3. Customize the layout by adding **text, images, and buttons**.
4. Use filters and search functions to refine displayed records.

2.2.2 App Settings and Environment

Every Power App operates within a defined **environment** and comes with customizable **settings** that influence its behavior. Understanding these elements ensures that your app runs **efficiently, securely, and meets user requirements**.

App Settings – Configuring Your Application

Power Apps provides several settings that allow you to control how your app functions. These settings can be accessed under the **File > Settings** menu.

Key App Settings

1. **General Settings** – Customize the app's name, icon, and description.
2. **Screen Size and Orientation** – Choose whether your app is designed for **phones, tablets, or desktops**.
3. **Data Connections** – Manage **databases, APIs, and third-party integrations**.
4. **Permissions and Security** – Control user access levels and authentication.
5. **Performance Optimization** – Adjust settings to enhance speed and responsiveness.

How to Configure App Settings

1. Click on **File** in Power Apps Studio.
2. Select **Settings** to open the configuration panel.
3. Adjust parameters such as **screen size, colors, and permissions**.
4. Save changes and preview your app to ensure everything works as expected.

Understanding Power Apps Environments

An **environment** in Power Apps is a space where apps, data, and resources are stored. It helps organize applications and ensures they operate within the right boundaries.

Types of Power Apps Environments

1. **Default Environment** – The standard space where all users start building apps.
2. **Sandbox Environment** – A testing space where developers can safely experiment without affecting live apps.
3. **Production Environment** – The final deployment area where fully developed apps are used by an organization.

How to Manage Your Environment

1. Open **Power Apps Admin Center** from the Microsoft Power Platform.
2. Navigate to **Environments** and select the one you want to manage.
3. Assign user roles and permissions to control access.
4. Configure data policies to protect sensitive information.

2.3 Creating a Simple App in Power Apps

Building an app might seem like a complex task, but **Power Apps** makes it surprisingly simple. With just a few steps, you can create an app that captures data, organizes information, and helps users interact with it efficiently. Whether you want to build a basic data entry form or a small business management tool, the process is **straightforward and user-friendly**.

Step 1: Accessing Power Apps Studio

Before creating an app, you need to **log in to Power Apps Studio**. This is the workspace where you will design and build your app.

How to Get Started

1. Open a **web browser** and go to the **Microsoft Power Apps** website.
2. Sign in with your **Microsoft account** or **work credentials**.
3. Once logged in, click on **"Create"** from the homepage.
4. Select the type of app you want to build:

- **Canvas App** – Allows you to design the app freely, just like a blank canvas.
- **Model-Driven App** – Provides a structured approach, focusing on business data.

1. For this guide, we will create a **Canvas App**, so click on **"Canvas app from blank"**.

43

Step 2: Choosing a Data Source

Apps in Power Apps **often interact with data**—whether it's stored in an Excel file, SharePoint list, or a database. Connecting your app to a data source ensures that users can **save, retrieve, and update information easily**.

How to Connect to a Data Source

1. In **Power Apps Studio**, click on the **Data** tab on the left panel.
2. Select **"Add data"** and choose your preferred data source:

- **Excel** – Ideal for storing structured data.
- **SharePoint** – Great for collaboration and team-based apps.
- **SQL Database** – Best for handling large amounts of data securely.

1. Follow the on-screen instructions to link your app to the data source.

Step 3: Designing the App Layout

Now that your app is connected to data, it's time to **design its appearance**. The layout determines how users interact with the app, so it should be **simple, clean, and easy to navigate**.

Adding Screens to Your App

1. Click on **"Insert"** in the toolbar.
2. Select **"New Screen"** to add a page where users will interact with the app.
3. Choose a screen type:

44

- **Blank** – Allows full customization.
- **List** – Displays data in a structured way.
- **Form** – Ideal for collecting input from users.

1. Drag and drop elements onto the screen, such as:

- **Labels** for titles and descriptions.
- **Buttons** to trigger actions.
- **Text Inputs** to allow users to enter information.
- **Dropdowns** for selecting options.

Step 4: Adding Functionality

An app isn't complete without functionality. This is where you define what happens when a user **clicks a button, enters data, or navigates between screens**.

Creating a Simple Data Entry Form

1. Insert a **Form Control** from the **Insert** menu.
2. Link it to your **data source** by selecting the source from the properties panel.
3. Add fields for users to fill out, such as **Name, Email, and Date of Birth**.
4. Insert a **Button Control** labeled **"Submit"**.
5. In the formula bar, set the button's function:

```
SubmitForm(Form1)
```

1. This command ensures that when users click **Submit**, their data is saved to the connected data source.

Adding Navigation Between Screens

If your app has multiple pages, users need a way to move between them. You can achieve this using buttons.

1. Insert a **Button Control** labeled **"Next"**.
2. In the **formula bar**, add the navigation function:

```
Navigate(Screen2, ScreenTransition.Fade)
```

1. This ensures users transition smoothly from one page to another.

Step 5: Testing and Publishing the App

Before making your app available to users, it's important to **test its functionality** and ensure everything works as expected.

How to Test Your App

1. Click on the **Preview (Play) Button** at the top-right corner of Power Apps Studio.
2. Interact with the app by **entering data, clicking buttons, and navigating through screens**.
3. If you notice any issues, adjust the settings or fix errors before proceeding.

How to Publish the App

1. Click on **File > Save and Publish**.
2. Give your app a **name** and add a **brief description**.
3. Click **"Publish this version"** to make the app live.
4. Share the app with **specific users or your entire organization**.

2.4 Basic Customizations: Themes, Fonts, and Colors

When building an app, functionality is essential, but **design** plays an equally important role. A well-designed app is not only **visually appealing** but also **enhances user experience** by making navigation smooth and interactions more intuitive. Power Apps provides a variety of **customization options**, allowing you to **personalize themes, fonts, and colors** to match your brand identity or preferences.

Step 1: Changing the Theme of Your App

Themes in Power Apps provide a **quick and easy way to style your app consistently**. Instead of manually selecting colors and fonts for each element, a theme applies a **cohesive design across the entire app**, ensuring a **polished and professional** look.

How to Apply a Theme

1. Open **Power Apps Studio** and select your app.
2. Click on the **"App"** section in the left-side panel.
3. Navigate to the **"Theme"** section in the properties pane.
4. Choose a pre-built theme from the available options.
5. Once selected, the theme automatically updates the app's **background, fonts, and button styles**.

Customizing a Theme

If the built-in themes do not meet your requirements, you can **create a custom theme** by manually selecting colors, fonts, and styling for each component.

1. Select the element you want to customize (e.g., buttons, text boxes, labels).
2. Open the **properties panel** and look for the **"Fill"** option to change the background color.
3. Adjust the **text color** by modifying the **"Color"** property.
4. Save the customizations and apply them to similar elements for **uniformity**.

Step 2: Modifying Fonts for Better Readability

Fonts play a critical role in how users perceive and interact with an app. A **clear and readable font** improves usability, while a stylish font can **enhance the app's aesthetic appeal**.

How to Change Fonts in Power Apps

1. Click on the **text element** you want to modify (e.g., labels, buttons, input fields).
2. In the **properties pane**, locate the **"Font"** option.
3. Choose from the available fonts provided by Power Apps.
4. Adjust the **font size** to ensure readability.
5. If necessary, make text **bold, italic, or underlined** using the formatting options.

Best Practices for Font Selection

- Use a **consistent font style** throughout the app to maintain a **professional look**.
- Keep body text between **14-16px** for easy readability.
- Headlines should be **larger and bold** to create a visual hierarchy.
- Avoid using too many font styles, as it can make the app look cluttered.

Step 3: Customizing Colors for a Unique Look

Colors define the **mood and personality** of an app. Choosing the right color scheme can **improve user engagement** and make interactions more intuitive. Power Apps allows you to **modify background colors, button colors, and text colors** to create a **visually appealing experience**.

How to Change Colors in Power Apps

1. Select an **element** (such as a button, text box, or screen background).
2. In the **properties panel**, look for the **"Fill"** option for background color.
3. Click on the **color picker** to select a color manually.
4. To change text color, modify the **"Color"** property.
5. Save changes and apply similar adjustments to maintain a **consistent look**.

Choosing the Right Color Scheme

- **Use complementary colors** to create contrast and highlight key features.
- **Dark text on a light background** is easier to read.
- **Accent colors** should be used sparingly for buttons and interactive elements.
- Ensure the colors are **accessible** to all users, including those with visual impairments.

Step 4: Saving and Applying Custom Styles Across the App

Once you have finalized your theme, fonts, and colors, you need to **apply them consistently** across the app to maintain a uniform look. Instead of modifying each element individually, you can use **global variables** to set standard styles for all components.

How to Create and Apply a Global Style

1. Go to the **"On Start"** property of your app.
2. Define a global variable for colors, such as:

```
Set(AppPrimaryColor, RGBA(0, 122, 255, 1))
```

1. Use this variable throughout the app by setting the **Fill** or **Color** property to **App Primary Color**.
2. Similarly, define font sizes and styles using variables to **maintain consistency**.

Chapter 3: Getting Your Data Right

Data is the backbone of any app. Without well-structured and reliable data, even the most visually stunning app will fail to deliver meaningful results. In Power Apps, understanding how data is stored, accessed, and used is essential for building an app that not only looks great but also functions smoothly. Whether you're working with a small database or integrating with complex systems, knowing how data sources work will help you **make informed decisions, improve performance, and ensure accuracy**.

3.1 Understanding Data Sources in Power Apps

What Are Data Sources?

A **data source** is where your app **stores, retrieves, and processes information**. It can be as simple as a list of customer names or as complex as a database that manages thousands of transactions in real time. Power Apps provides flexibility by allowing you to connect to various **data sources**, enabling you to create apps that meet different needs.

These data sources can be categorized into:

1. **Cloud-based storage** – Examples include SharePoint, Microsoft Dataverse, OneDrive, and Excel files stored online.
2. **Databases** – SQL Server, Azure SQL, MySQL, and Oracle.
3. **Online services (APIs and connectors)** – Power Apps can pull data from platforms like Microsoft 365, Salesforce, or Google Sheets.
4. **Local storage and on-premises data** – If your data is stored in an internal server or desktop database, Power Apps can connect to it using **gateways**.

Each type of data source has **unique strengths and limitations**. Choosing the right one depends on **what your app needs to do**.

Step 1: Connecting to a Data Source in Power Apps

Before you can use data in your app, you need to **connect to a data source**. Power Apps makes this process simple by offering pre-built connectors for many popular platforms.

How to Add a Data Source

1. Open **Power Apps Studio** and select your app.
2. Click on the **"Data"** tab in the left-hand menu.
3. Choose **"Add data"** to open the list of available data sources.
4. Search for and select the data source you want to use (e.g., SharePoint, SQL Server, or Excel).

5. Follow the prompts to **sign in and grant access** to your data.
6. Once connected, you will see the data source appear in the **"Data"** section.

After adding a data source, Power Apps allows you to **bind it to different controls**, such as tables, forms, and dropdown lists, making it easy to display and manage data.

Step 2: Choosing the Right Data Source for Your App

Selecting the right data source depends on **how your app will be used and what kind of data it needs to handle**. Below are a few key considerations:

- **For small-scale apps with simple lists** → Use Excel or SharePoint lists.
- **For enterprise apps with structured data** → Dataverse or SQL Server provides more stability.
- **For real-time data retrieval from other platforms** → Use APIbased connectors like Salesforce or Microsoft 365.
- **For offline capabilities** → Consider using local storage or cached data to allow users to work without an internet connection.

Choosing the **right data source** ensures your app runs **efficiently, loads data quickly, and remains scalable** as your needs grow.

Step 3: Working with Different Types of Data in Power Apps

Power Apps supports various types of data, such as:

1. **Text data** – Names, addresses, descriptions.
2. **Numerical data** – Prices, product quantities, employee salaries.
3. **Dates and times** – Appointment schedules, deadlines, timestamps.
4. **Boolean (True/False) values** – Used for checkboxes and status updates.
5. **Images and files** – Profile pictures, invoices, uploaded documents.

Binding Data to Controls

Once a data source is connected, you need to **link it to controls** in your app so that users can view, edit, and interact with the data.

- **Tables and Galleries** → Display multiple records from your data source.
- **Forms** → Allow users to input and update data.
- **Dropdowns and Combo Boxes** → Filter and select values dynamically.
- **Buttons and Actions** → Trigger data updates, submissions, and automation.

Understanding how to **bind data to these controls** makes your app interactive and user-friendly.

Step 4: Keeping Your Data Secure and Reliable

Managing data correctly isn't just about storing information—it's about ensuring **security, accuracy, and performance**. Here's how to keep your data safe and functional:

- **Restrict user access** – Only allow authorized users to edit or view certain records.
- **Validate data inputs** – Use rules to prevent incorrect or incomplete entries.
- **Regularly update data sources** – Keep information current to avoid outdated records.
- **Optimize performance** – Avoid pulling too much data at once; instead, use filters and queries.

By following these best practices, your app will remain **secure, efficient, and easy to maintain**.

3.2 Connecting to Data: SharePoint, Excel, SQL Server, and More

Data is at the heart of every successful Power Apps application. Without a proper data connection, your app is just a collection of buttons and screens with no real functionality. To create a dynamic, responsive, and efficient app, you need to **connect it to reliable data sources** where information is stored and retrieved.

Power Apps allows you to **seamlessly connect** to a variety of data sources, including **SharePoint, Excel, SQL Server, and many more**.

Each of these sources serves a different purpose, and selecting the right one ensures **smooth performance and an enhanced user experience**.

This section will guide you through **understanding different data sources, how to connect them, and best practices for working with them effectively**.

Understanding Data Sources in Power Apps

A **data source** is where your app **stores, retrieves, and processes data**. Power Apps supports various data sources, making it easy to build flexible apps that **meet specific business needs**. Below are some of the most commonly used data sources and what they are best suited for:

1. **SharePoint** – Ideal for storing lists, documents, and structured information.
2. **Excel (Stored in OneDrive or SharePoint)** – Suitable for small datasets and lightweight apps.
3. **SQL Server** – Best for handling large-scale structured data, offering strong security and performance.
4. **Dataverse** – Microsoft's cloud-based data storage solution that integrates deeply with Power Apps and other Microsoft services.
5. **Other Third-Party Services** – Power Apps also supports external services like Salesforce, Google Sheets, and more through connectors.

Choosing the right data source depends on **how complex your data is, how frequently it updates, and how many users will access it**.

Step 1: Adding a Data Source to Your App

Connecting a data source to Power Apps is a simple process that allows your app to interact with real-world data. Follow these steps to **establish a data connection**:

1. **Open Power Apps Studio** and go to the app where you want to add a data source.
2. Click on the **"Data"** tab from the left panel.
3. Click on **"Add data"**, which will open a list of available connectors.
4. Select your preferred data source (e.g., SharePoint, Excel, or SQL Server).
5. Follow the authentication steps, such as **logging into your Microsoft account or entering your database credentials**.
6. Once successfully connected, your data source will appear under the **"Data"** section, ready to be used within your app.

After completing these steps, your app can now **pull, display, and update data in real-time**.

Step 2: Connecting to Specific Data Sources

Different data sources require slightly different connection steps. Below is a breakdown of how to connect some of the most popular ones:

1. Connecting to SharePoint

SharePoint is widely used for storing structured lists and documents. It's a great option for businesses that **already rely on Microsoft 365**.
How to Connect Power Apps to SharePoint:

- Select **SharePoint** from the list of available data sources.
- Enter the **URL of your SharePoint site**.
- Choose the **list** you want to connect to (e.g., "Customer Orders" or "Employee Directory").
- Click **"Connect"**, and Power Apps will import your list.

Now, your app can **read and update** SharePoint list data directly.

2. Connecting to Excel (Stored in OneDrive or SharePoint)

Excel is a simple yet powerful tool for managing data. When stored in **OneDrive or SharePoint**, it becomes a convenient data source for Power Apps.
How to Connect Power Apps to an Excel File:

- Select **OneDrive for Business** or **SharePoint** as your data source.
- Navigate to the location where your **Excel file is stored**.
- Choose the correct file and **select the table inside it**.
- Click **"Connect"**, and the data from your Excel table will now be available in Power Apps.

To ensure smooth performance, always use **structured tables** within your Excel file rather than raw cell ranges.

3. Connecting to SQL Server

SQL Server is a powerful option for handling **large datasets and complex business applications**.

   How to Connect Power Apps to SQL Server:

- Choose **SQL Server** from the list of data sources.
- Enter your **server name and database name**.
- Select the **authentication method** (e.g., Windows authentication or SQL authentication).
- Click **"Connect"** and select the tables you need for your app.

SQL Server provides **better scalability, security, and performance** than Excel or SharePoint, making it the preferred choice for enterprise apps.

Step 3: Best Practices for Working with Data Sources

Connecting your app to a data source is only the first step. To keep your app **fast, secure, and reliable**, follow these best practices:

1. **Use Delegation** – When working with large datasets, ensure that Power Apps **delegates queries to the data source** instead of loading everything at once. This prevents performance issues.
2. **Keep Data Sources Simple** – Avoid excessive columns or unnecessary data fields. This speeds up data retrieval and improves efficiency.
3. **Secure Your Data** – Implement role-based access controls, so users only see data they are authorized to view.
4. **Limit Data Calls** – Instead of constantly retrieving data, use caching methods to reduce network traffic and improve

responsive

5. **Regularly Maintain Your Data** – Clean up old records, remove unused columns, and update permissions to keep your database organized.

3.3 Creating and Managing Dataverse Tables

Data is the backbone of any application, and in Power Apps, **Dataverse** provides a secure, structured, and scalable way to store and manage data. Whether you are building a simple app or a complex enterprise solution, **organizing your data effectively** is crucial for performance and ease of use.

Dataverse acts as a **centralized data storage solution**, allowing businesses to **store, organize, and securely share information across multiple applications**. Unlike traditional spreadsheets or databases, Dataverse offers **predefined tables, advanced security, and seamless integration with Microsoft services**.

Understanding Dataverse Tables

A **table** in Dataverse is similar to a spreadsheet or a database table—it **stores records, organizes data into fields, and ensures structured management**. Each table consists of:

- **Columns (Fields)** – Define the type of data each record will store, such as text, numbers, dates, or choices.
- **Rows (Records)** – Individual data entries within the table.

- **Relationships** – Connect different tables to create meaningful data links.

Dataverse provides two types of tables:

1. **Standard Tables** – Predefined by Microsoft to handle common business data like contacts, accounts, and transactions.
2. **Custom Tables** – Created by users to **store unique business specific information** that does not fit into the standard table categories.

Choosing the right table type is essential for maintaining **data accuracy and efficiency**.

Step 1: Creating a Dataverse Table

To store data effectively in Power Apps, you need to **set up a new table** in Dataverse. Follow these steps to create one:

1. **Open Power Apps Studio** and navigate to the **Dataverse section** from the left panel.
2. Click on **"Tables"**, then select **"New Table"** to create a custom data structure.
3. Enter a **Table Name** that clearly represents the type of data it will hold (e.g., "Customer Orders" or "Employee Records").
4. Add a **Primary Column** – This serves as the unique identifier for each record in the table.
5. Click **"Save"** to create the table.

At this stage, your Dataverse table is ready, but it still needs **columns to define what data will be stored**.

Step 2: Adding Columns to Your Table

Columns define what type of data your table can hold. A well-structured table with **clear column definitions** ensures smooth app functionality.

1. Open the newly created table and navigate to the **Columns section**.
2. Click **"Add Column"** and enter a **Name** (e.g., "Customer Name" or "Order Date").
3. Select a **Data Type**:

- **Text** – For names, descriptions, and general information.
- **Number** – For quantities, prices, or ID numbers.
- **Date and Time** – For storing appointment dates or timestamps.
- **Choice** – For predefined options like order status ("Pending," "Completed," etc.).

1. Configure **additional settings**, such as making the column required or setting default values.
2. Click **"Save"**, and the new column will be added to your table.

Repeating this process allows you to **build a fully functional table** that stores data efficiently.

Step 3: Managing Dataverse Tables

Once your table is set up, it is important to **maintain, update, and optimize** it over time. Proper management helps keep data clean, organized, and secure.

Editing Existing Tables

- Navigate to the **Dataverse section** and open the table you want to modify.
- To rename a column, click on it, update the name, and save changes.
- If you need to remove unnecessary columns, select the column and click **"Delete"** (ensure it's not in use).

Creating Relationships Between Tables

For more complex apps, you may need to **connect multiple tables**. This allows data to be linked, reducing redundancy and improving efficiency.

1. Open your table and go to the **Relationships section**.
2. Click **"New Relationship"** and choose a table to connect it to.
3. Select the **relationship type**:

- **One-to-One** – Each record in Table A links to one record in Table B.
- **One-to-Many** – One record in Table A can connect to multiple records in Table B.
- **Many-to-Many** – Records in both tables can have multiple connections.

1. Click **"Save"**, and your tables are now linked.

This ensures **efficient data management** by eliminating duplicate records and improving reporting accuracy.

Step 4: Setting Up Security and Permissions

Data security is crucial, especially when multiple users interact with the same dataset. Dataverse offers **role-based access control**, ensuring that only authorized users can view, edit, or delete data.

Configuring Table Security:

1. Navigate to the **Security settings** within Dataverse.
2. Assign roles to users or teams (e.g., Admin, Editor, Viewer).
3. Define permissions for each role:

- **Full Access** – Can add, update, and delete records.
- **Read-Only** – Can view but not modify data.
- **Limited Access** – Can access only specific columns or records.

1. Save changes to apply the security settings.

By managing security settings properly, you can **protect sensitive information while allowing collaboration**.

Best Practices for Managing Dataverse Tables

To keep your Dataverse tables optimized and effective, follow these **best practices**:

1. **Use Consistent Naming Conventions** – Avoid generic names like "Table1." Instead, use descriptive names such as "Employee Records" for clarity.
2. **Minimize Unnecessary Columns** – Keep only the essential data fields to improve performance.

3. **Regularly Review and Clean Up Data** – Delete outdated records and unnecessary columns to keep the database organized.
4. **Enable Auditing** – Track changes to records to monitor data updates.
5. **Back Up Important Data** – Prevent accidental data loss by setting up regular backups.

3.4 Filtering and Sorting Data in Power Apps

When working with large sets of data, **finding the right information quickly and efficiently** is essential. Whether you are managing customer records, tracking inventory, or handling employee details, **sorting and filtering data** allows users to focus on what matters most.

Power Apps provides powerful tools to **organize, refine, and display data** in a way that enhances user experience and improves decision-making. By properly applying filters and sorting, you can create an application that is both efficient and user-friendly.

Understanding Filtering and Sorting in Power Apps

What Is Filtering?

Filtering **narrows down data** based on specific conditions. For example, if you have a list of employees, you can filter it to **show only employees from a specific department or those hired within the last year**.

What Is Sorting?

Sorting **arranges data in a specific order**—either **ascending (A-Z, 1-10, earliest to latest)** or **descending (Z-A, 10-1, latest to earliest)**. For instance, you might want to **sort orders by date** so the most recent ones appear at the top.

By combining both **filtering and sorting**, you can create a structured, well-organized display of information that allows users to find what they need with ease.

Step 1: Filtering Data in Power Apps

Filtering helps users **focus on relevant records** by setting conditions that determine what should be displayed. Power Apps uses the **Filter()** function to achieve this.

How to Apply a Filter:

1. **Open Power Apps Studio** and navigate to the screen where you want to display filtered data.
2. Click on the **Gallery Control** (or a table, dropdown, or combo box where the data will be displayed).
3. In the **Items** property of the control, enter the **Filter()** function:

```
Filter(DataSource, Condition)
```

1. Replace **DataSource** with your actual data source, and **Condition** with the criteria you want to filter by.

Example Scenarios for Filtering:

- **Showing customers from a specific city:**

```
Filter(Customers, City = "New York")
```

- This will display only customers who are from New York.
- **Filtering employees hired after 2022:**

```
Filter(Employees, HireDate > DateValue("01/01/2022"))
```

- This will show only employees hired after January 1, 2022.
- **Displaying only active orders:**

```
Filter(Orders, Status = "Active")
```

- This ensures only orders marked as "Active" are visible.

By applying filters, your users can **quickly locate the information they need without having to scroll through unnecessary data**.

Step 2: Sorting Data in Power Apps

Sorting helps users **view data in an orderly fashion**, making it easier to analyze trends and locate specific records. Power Apps uses the **Sort()** function to arrange records.

How to Apply Sorting:

1. **Select the control** displaying your data (such as a gallery or table).
2. Click on the **Items** property and enter the **Sort()** function:

```
Sort(DataSource, ColumnName, SortOrder)
```

1. Replace **DataSource** with your actual data source, **ColumnName** with the field you want to sort by, and **SortOrder** with either **Ascending** or **Descending**.

Example Scenarios for Sorting:

- **Sorting products by price (low to high):**

```
Sort(Products, Price, Ascending)
```

- This arranges the product list starting from the lowest price.
- **Sorting employees by name (A-Z):**

70

```
Sort(Employees, Name, Ascending)
```

- This displays employees in alphabetical order.
- **Sorting orders by the most recent date first:**

```
Sort(Orders, OrderDate, Descending)
```

- This ensures that the latest orders appear at the top.

Sorting ensures that data remains **organized and easy to navigate**, helping users make faster, more informed decisions.

Step 3: Combining Filtering and Sorting

For the best user experience, **combine filtering and sorting** so that users not only see relevant data but also find it in a logical order.

How to Combine Both Functions:

1. In the **Items** property of your control, use the **SortByColumns()** function along with **Filter()**:

```
SortByColumns(Filter(DataSource, Condition), ColumnName,
SortOrder)
```

1. Modify it to match your specific data source and conditions.

Example Scenarios for Combined Sorting and Filtering:

- **Displaying only "Active" customers, sorted by name (A-Z):**

```
SortByColumns(Filter(Customers, Status = "Active"), Name,
Ascending)
```

- **Showing employees hired after 2022, sorted by hiring date (latest first):**

```
SortByColumns(Filter(Employees, HireDate >
DateValue("01/01/2022")), HireDate, Descending)
```

- **Displaying completed orders from the last 30 days, sorted by total amount (high to low):**

```
SortByColumns(Filter(Orders, Status = "Completed" &&
OrderDate >= Today() 30), TotalAmount, Descending)
```

By applying both filtering and sorting, you ensure that **your users only see the most relevant and well-organized data,** making interactions with the app smoother and more efficient.

Step 4: Creating a User-Friendly Filtering and Sorting Experience

While adding filtering and sorting through formulas is useful, giving users **interactive controls** allows them to **customize their own view of the data**.

Adding a Dropdown for Filtering:

1. Insert a **Dropdown control** for users to select a filter option.
2. Set the **Items** property of the dropdown:

```
["All", "New York", "Los Angeles", "Chicago"]
```

1. Update the **Gallery Items** property to filter based on the dropdown selection:

```
If(Dropdown1.Selected.Value = "All", Customers,
Filter(Customers, City = Dropdown1.Selected.Value))
```

Adding Buttons for Sorting:

1. Insert two **Button controls** labeled **"Sort A-Z"** and **"Sort Z-A"**.
2. Set their **On Select** property to update a variable:

73

```
UpdateContext({sortOrder: Ascending})
```

1. for A-Z sorting, and

```
UpdateContext({sortOrder: Descending})
```

1. for Z-A sorting.
2. Modify the **Gallery Items** property:

```
Sort(Customers, Name, sortOrder)
```

These interactive controls provide a **better user experience** by letting users **choose how they want their data displayed** instead of relying on fixed filters and sorting.

3.5 Tips for Data Connections in Power Apps

Data is the foundation of any app. The way you connect to and manage your data determines how smoothly your application functions. **Power Apps** allows seamless integration with various data sources such as **SharePoint, Excel, SQL Server, Dataverse, and more**, giving you the flexibility to build powerful applications.

However, simply connecting to data is not enough. To create an app that is **efficient, reliable, and user-friendly**, it's essential to follow best practices for data connections.

1. Choose the Right Data Source

The first step in a successful app is selecting the appropriate data source. Each source has its own strengths, and the choice depends on **your specific needs and the complexity of your application**.

Best Practices for Choosing a Data Source:

- **For small-scale apps with simple data needs:** Use **Excel or SharePoint** for ease of use.
- **For apps handling large amounts of structured data:** Use **Dataverse or SQL Server** for better performance and scalability.
- **For real-time updates and complex business logic: Dataverse** is the best option, as it provides advanced data management features.

By selecting the **right data source from the beginning,** you ensure your app runs efficiently and avoids performance issues in the future.

2. Maintain a Stable Data Connection

A weak or unstable data connection can **disrupt your app's functionality, causing delays, errors, or even crashes**. To prevent these issues, you need to ensure that your data connections are well managed.

How to Maintain a Reliable Data Connection:

- **Use cloud-based data sources** such as SharePoint, Dataverse, or SQL Server to ensure accessibility from any location.
- **Avoid local Excel files** stored on personal computers, as they

can cause connection issues.

- **Limit the number of connections in a single app** to avoid slow performance.
- **Use cached data** where possible to reduce the number of calls to external data sources.

By following these steps, your app remains stable and functional, even when handling large amounts of data.

3. Optimize Performance with Delegation

When working with large data sets, Power Apps **does not load all records at once**. Instead, it retrieves data in small batches to improve performance. This is called **delegation**—allowing Power Apps to push data processing to the data source rather than handling it within the app itself.

How to Use Delegation Effectively:

- **Use Delegable Functions** such as Filter(), Sort(), and Search() when working with large data sources.
- **Avoid Non-Delegable Formulas**, as they force Power Apps to pull all records into memory, slowing down performance.
- **Check the Delegation Warning Icon**, which appears when a formula is not fully supported.

By ensuring your app uses **delegable queries**, you keep it running smoothly, even when dealing with thousands of records.

4. Secure Your Data Connections

Security is a crucial aspect of any application, especially when dealing with **sensitive user information, financial records, or confidential company data**. Without proper security measures, your data could be exposed to unauthorized users.

Ways to Secure Your Data Connections:

- **Use Role-Based Access Control (RBAC):** Assign permissions based on user roles to restrict access to certain data.
- **Avoid storing sensitive data in Excel or unsecured sources:** Use **Dataverse or SQL Server**, which provide encryption and security layers.
- **Enable Multi-Factor Authentication (MFA):** Adding an extra layer of security helps protect your app from unauthorized access.
- **Use Power Apps Environment Security:** If your organization has multiple apps, managing security at the environment level ensures that sensitive data remains protected.

By implementing strong security practices, you protect both your application and the users who rely on it.

5. Reduce Unnecessary Data Loads

Fetching **too much data at once** can slow down your app and lead to performance issues. Instead of loading entire tables, retrieve only the necessary records that users need at any given time.

How to Reduce Data Load for Better Performance:

- **Use the Filter() function** to retrieve only relevant records instead of loading all data.
- **Load data on demand:** Instead of pulling all records at once, use galleries and search functions to fetch only what is needed.
- **Limit the number of columns retrieved:** Select only the essential fields rather than loading entire tables.

By keeping your data load minimal, your app remains **fast, responsive, and easy to use**.

6. Use Collections for Offline Support

If your users work in areas with **poor or no internet connectivity**, ensuring they can access data offline is critical. Power Apps allows you to **store data locally using Collections**, so users can still interact with the app even when offline.

How to Enable Offline Support:

1. **Store Data in a Collection:**

```
ClearCollect(MyCollection, DataSource)
```

1. This saves a snapshot of data for offline access.
2. **Use the Collection Instead of the Live Data Source:**

```
Gallery.Items = MyCollection
```

1. This ensures the app works offline using the stored data.
2. **Sync Data When Connectivity Returns:**
3. When the device reconnects to the internet, update the data source:

```
Patch(DataSource, MyCollection)
```

1. This pushes offline changes back to the main database.

By implementing offline support, you **enhance reliability and usability**, allowing users to work without interruptions.

7. Test and Monitor Data Connections Regularly

Even after setting up your data connections, it's important to **continuously test and monitor their performance**. Unexpected issues can arise, and regular testing ensures that everything functions smoothly.

Steps to Test and Monitor Data Connections:

- **Use Power Apps Monitor** to check for errors and slow queries.
- **Test in different network conditions** to ensure the app performs well even with slow internet.
- **Check for Delegation Warnings** to optimize performance.
- **Regularly review security settings** to ensure user access

remains controlled.

Frequent testing helps **identify potential issues before they impact users**, keeping your app reliable and efficient.

Chapter 4: Canvas Apps

4.1 Introduction to Canvas Apps

Technology has transformed the way businesses and individuals build solutions, making app development more accessible than ever. **Canvas Apps** in Power Apps offer a way to create **custom applications** that meet specific needs—without requiring complex coding skills. Whether you want to design a simple tool for personal use or a fully functional business application, **Canvas Apps put the power in your hands.**

What Are Canvas Apps?

Think of **Canvas Apps** as a **blank canvas** where you can design an application from scratch. You have complete control over how your app looks, how it functions, and how users interact with it. You can **drag and drop elements**, connect to multiple data sources, and customize every detail to fit your exact needs.

Unlike **Model-Driven Apps**, which are structured around data models, **Canvas Apps** allow for **creative freedom**. This makes them perfect for applications where user experience and layout customization are a priority.

Why Choose Canvas Apps?

- **Easy to Use:** No coding experience? No problem! The drag and drop interface makes it simple to design and build apps.
- **Highly Customizable:** Unlike prebuilt templates, you control every button, field, and function in your app.
- **Connects to Various Data Sources:** Use SharePoint, Excel, SQL Server, and many other services to power your app.
- **Works on Any Device:** Canvas Apps function on mobile phones, tablets, and desktops, ensuring accessibility.
- **Faster Development:** Instead of months of coding, you can build a functional app in hours or days.

With these benefits, **Canvas Apps allow anyone—regardless of technical background—to create powerful, user-friendly applications.**

How Canvas Apps Work

At its core, a **Canvas App** is built in a way that feels familiar— like designing a presentation in PowerPoint. You **place elements (controls)** onto a blank screen, define how they behave, and connect them to data sources that provide the necessary information.

Key Components of a Canvas App:

1. **Screens:** These are the pages of your app. An app can have multiple screens, each serving a different purpose (e.g., home screen, form submission screen, reports screen).
2. **Controls:** Buttons, text fields, dropdown menus, images, and charts—everything that users interact with.
3. **Data Connections:** The backbone of any app. You can connect to various databases, cloud services, or even APIs.
4. **Formulas:** Power Apps uses formulas (similar to Excel) to define how controls behave and interact with data.
5. **Variables:** These store temporary values and help manage user actions within the app.

By combining these components, **you can create dynamic and interactive apps that perform real-world functions efficiently.**

Steps to Build Your First Canvas App

If you're ready to explore Canvas Apps, the best way to learn is by building one yourself. Follow these simple steps to create your first app:

Step 1: Open Power Apps Studio

Power Apps Studio is the **design environment** where you create and edit Canvas Apps. To access it:

1. Sign in to Power Apps.
2. Click on **"Create"** from the home screen.
3. Select **Canvas App** and choose either **Tablet Layout** or **Phone**

Layout, depending on your needs.

Step 2: Add a Data Source

Your app needs data to function. To connect it to a source:

1. Click on **"Data"** in the left panel.
2. Choose **"Add data"** and select a service like SharePoint, Excel, or SQL Server.
3. Follow the prompts to authenticate and connect your data.

Step 3: Design Your Screens

Now, it's time to **build the visual structure of your app.**

1. Click on **"Insert"** to add controls such as labels, text inputs, and buttons.
2. Arrange them on the screen to create a user-friendly layout.
3. Customize fonts, colors, and sizes to match your preferred design.

Step 4: Define Functionality with Formulas

Formulas in Power Apps **control what happens when users interact with your app.** For example:

- To **navigate between screens**, use:

```
Navigate(Screen2, ScreenTransition.Fade)
```

- To **save data to a database**, use:

```
Patch(DataSource, Defaults(DataSource), {Title:
TextInput1.Text})
```

These formulas bring your app to life by handling user actions.

Step 5: Test and Publish Your App

Before sharing your app with others:

1. Click **"Preview"** to test functionality.
2. Fix any issues or errors.
3. Click **"Save"** and then **"Publish"** to make the app available to users.

Congratulations! You've built your first Canvas App.

Best Practices for Creating Effective Canvas Apps

To make sure your Canvas App is **efficient, user-friendly, and scalable**, keep these best practices in mind:

- **Start with a Plan:** Sketch your app layout and flow before building.
- **Keep the Design Simple:** Avoid cluttered screens and too many controls.
- **Optimize Performance:** Limit data connections and use delegation for large datasets.
- **Test on Different Devices:** Ensure your app works well on

mobile, tablet, and desktop.

- **Focus on User Experience:** Your app should be easy to navigate and intuitive to use.

By following these principles, **you can build a high-quality Canvas App that meets both personal and business needs.**

4.2 Creating a Canvas App from Scratch

Building an app from scratch may seem overwhelming, but with **Canvas Apps in Power Apps,** it becomes a smooth and rewarding process. Whether you're automating tasks, improving business operations, or creating a tool for personal use, **Canvas Apps give you complete control over the design and functionality.**

Understanding the Power of a Canvas App

A **Canvas App** is like a blank sheet where you design and develop an application **exactly how you want it.** You can choose what appears on the screen, where buttons go, how users interact with the app, and what happens when they press a button.

The best part? **You don't need advanced technical skills.** With a simple **drag-and-drop interface,** you can add and arrange elements effortlessly. Whether you're connecting to data, designing forms, or creating navigation menus, **Canvas Apps offer unmatched flexibility.**

Step-by-Step Guide to Creating a Canvas App

Follow these instructions to build a **fully functional Canvas App from scratch.**

Step 1: Open Power Apps Studio

1. **Sign in** to Power Apps at the Microsoft Power Apps portal.
2. Click **"Create"** from the home screen.
3. Choose **"Canvas App"** and select whether you want a **Tablet** or **Phone Layout.**
4. Give your app a meaningful **name** and click **"Create."**

Now, your blank **Canvas App is ready to be designed.**

Step 2: Add a Data Source (Optional, but Recommended)

Most apps need data to function. You can connect your app to a database, cloud service, or Excel file.
   To connect to a data source:

1. Click **"Data"** in the left panel.
2. Select **"Add data."**
3. Choose a source such as **SharePoint, SQL Server, Excel, or Dataverse.**
4. Authenticate and follow the setup prompts.

Once connected, your app can **retrieve and store data dynamically.**

Step 3: Design the App Layout

Now that your app is ready, it's time to **add screens and controls** to shape how it looks and functions.

1. **Create Screens:**

- Click **"New Screen"** to add different sections like a **Home Screen, Form Screen, or List Screen.**

1. **Insert Controls:**

- Use the **"Insert"** tab to add **buttons, labels, text inputs, images, or dropdowns.**

1. **Customize the Appearance:**

- Resize and position elements to **improve user experience.**
- Modify colors, fonts, and styles to **match your vision.**
- Add **logos and background images** for a professional touch.

Your app is now taking shape, but it needs functionality.

Step 4: Add Functionality Using Formulas

Power Apps uses simple **formulas** (like Excel) to define what happens when users **click buttons, enter data, or move between screens.**
   Here are some key formulas to make your app interactive:

1. **Navigate to Another Screen:**

```
Navigate(Screen2, ScreenTransition.Fade)
```

1. This makes the app transition smoothly between screens.
2. **Submit a Form to a Data Source:**

```
SubmitForm(EditForm1)
```

1. This command **saves user-entered data.**
2. **Show or Hide Elements Based on Conditions:**

```
If(Toggle1.Value=true, Label1.Visible=true,
Label1.Visible=false)
```

1. This ensures that elements appear only when needed.

By combining these formulas, you **bring your app to life.**

Step 5: Test Your App

Before publishing, **testing is crucial** to ensure everything runs smoothly.

1. Click the **"Preview"** button in Power Apps Studio.
2. Interact with the app: **Click buttons, enter data, and switch between screens.**

3. If something isn't working correctly, **adjust formulas or control settings.**

Once satisfied, your app is ready to go live.

Step 6: Save, Publish, and Share Your App

When your app is complete, it's time to make it available for others.

1. Click **"File" > "Save"** to store your progress.
2. Select **"Publish"** to make it accessible to users.
3. Share the app with your team or organization by adjusting **user permissions.**

Your **Canvas App is now live**, and users can access it from their **desktop, tablet, or mobile device.**

Best Practices for a Well-Designed Canvas App

To ensure your app is **efficient, user-friendly, and scalable**, follow these best practices:

- **Plan Before You Build:** Sketch your app layout and workflow before opening Power Apps.
- **Keep the Interface Simple:** Avoid cluttered screens and excessive buttons.
- **Use Consistent Design Elements:** Ensure colors, fonts, and buttons follow a uniform style.
- **Optimize for Performance:** Reduce unnecessary data connections and large image files.
- **Test on Multiple Devices:** Verify functionality on both mobile

and desktop screens.

4.3 Working with Canvas App Components

Labels, Text Inputs, and Buttons

When creating a **Canvas App**, understanding its core components is essential. These elements form the **building blocks** of your app, allowing users to interact with it in a smooth and meaningful way.

Understanding Canvas App Components

Think of a **Canvas App** as a digital workspace where you place elements to create an interactive experience.

- **Labels** display important information.
- **Text Inputs** allow users to enter data.
- **Buttons** trigger actions and responses.

By combining these components, you **bring your app to life**, ensuring a smooth and efficient user experience.

Step-by-Step Guide to Using Labels, Text Inputs, and Buttons

Step 1: Adding a Label

Labels are used to **display static or dynamic text** in your app. They help users understand instructions, titles, or results.

1. Open **Power Apps Studio** and go to your Canvas App.
2. Click the **"Insert"** tab and select **"Label."**
3. Drag the Label onto your screen and position it as needed.
4. Customize the text by selecting the **"Text"** property in the right panel.
5. Change the font size, color, or style to enhance readability.

Example: If you want a greeting message, set the Text property like this:

```
"Welcome to My App!"
```

Step 2: Adding a Text Input Field

A **Text Input** field allows users to type information, such as names, emails, or comments.

1. Click **"Insert"** and choose **"Text Input."**
2. Place it on your screen where users will enter data.
3. Adjust the size and position for a neat layout.
4. Set a placeholder text to guide users (e.g., "Enter your name here").

To display what the user types, link the **Text Input** to a **Label**:

```
Label1.Text = TextInput1.Text
```

Now, whatever the user enters in the **Text Input**, the **Label** will display it in real time.

Step 3: Adding a Button to Trigger an Action

A **Button** is an interactive element that performs an action when clicked. It can **save data, navigate screens, or trigger notifications.**

1. Click **"Insert"** and select **"Button."**
2. Place it below your Text Input field.
3. Change the button's **text** to something meaningful, like **"Submit"** or **"Save."**
4. Modify the **size, color, and font** to match your app's theme.

To make the button display a welcome message when clicked, add this formula to its **On Select** property:

```
Label1.Text = "Hello, " & TextInput1.Text & "!"
```

Now, when a user enters their name and clicks the button, the **Label** will greet them with a personalized message.

Customizing Labels, Text Inputs, and Buttons

To make your app more **visually appealing and user-friendly**, customize each component:

- **Labels:** Adjust **font size, color, and alignment** for better visibility.

- **Text Inputs:** Set **borders, background colors, and default text** to guide users.
- **Buttons:** Change **shape, color, and hover effects** for an interactive experience.

Example of a **styled button** using a formula in its **Fill** property:

```
If(Button1.Pressed, RGBA(0, 122, 255, 1), RGBA(255, 0, 0,
1))
```

This changes the button color when clicked.

Bringing It All Together

Let's create a simple **form** using these three components:

1. **Add a Label** at the top: "Enter Your Name:"
2. **Insert a Text Input** field below it.
3. **Place a Button** with the text **"Greet Me."**
4. **Set the Button's On Select property** to display a welcome message in a **new Label.**

Now, when users type their name and press the button, they receive a **personalized greeting** instantly.

Best Practices for Using Canvas App Components

To build a smooth and engaging app, keep these tips in mind:

- **Keep it simple:** Avoid cluttered screens with too many labels or buttons.

- **Use clear instructions:** Labels should **guide users, not confuse them.**
- **Ensure responsiveness:** Make sure text inputs and buttons **work well on mobile and desktop.**
- **Enhance accessibility:** Use **contrasting colors and large text** for better readability.

Test frequently: Always check if buttons perform the correct actions.

4.4 Implementing Layouts and Navigation in Canvas Apps

Creating an effective **Canvas App** goes beyond adding buttons and text fields. The way your app is structured—the layout and navigation—determines how smoothly users can interact with it. A well-designed app should be **intuitive, visually appealing, and easy to navigate.**

Understanding Layouts in a Canvas App

A **layout** refers to how different elements are arranged on the screen. A clear and structured design ensures users can **quickly find what they need** without feeling overwhelmed.

Types of Layouts

1. **Single-Screen Layout** – All features are on one screen, suitable for simple apps.
2. **Multi-Screen Layout** – Different screens organize various functions, used in complex apps.
3. **Tab-Based Layout** – Users switch between sections using tabs.
4. **Header and Footer Layout** – Keeps navigation and key options visible at all times.

Choosing the right layout depends on the **purpose of your app and the amount of content** it needs to display.

Step-by-Step Guide to Implementing Layouts

Step 1: Choosing the Right Screen Type

1. Open **Power Apps Studio** and create a new **Canvas App.**
2. In the **Tree View**, click **Screens** and select **"New Screen."**
3. Choose from built-in templates like **Blank, List, or Form Screen.**
4. Arrange elements logically—important actions should be easy to access.

Step 2: Structuring the Layout with Containers

Containers help align elements properly. Use them to ensure your app looks professional and functions smoothly on **both desktop and mobile.**

1. Click **"Insert"** and select **"Container"** from the Layout section.

2. Drag it onto the screen and adjust its size.
3. Inside the container, place **buttons, labels, and input fields.**
4. Group related elements together to make the app easier to use.

Example: If designing a form, keep the **title, input fields, and submit button** aligned in one structured container.

Step 3: Adjusting the Layout for Different Devices

Users may access your app from **phones, tablets, or desktops.** To ensure a smooth experience across all screens:

1. Click **"App Settings"** and go to **Display.**
2. Choose between **Portrait (Mobile) or Landscape (Tablet/Desktop).**
3. Use the **Flexible Height and Width** properties to make elements adjust automatically.

A responsive design means your app will look good **on any screen size.**

Setting Up Navigation in Canvas Apps

Navigation allows users to **move between screens** smoothly. Without proper navigation, users may struggle to find information or complete tasks.

Step-by-Step Guide to Adding Navigation

Step 1: Adding Navigation Buttons

1. Click **"Insert"** and choose **"Button."**
2. Place the button at a convenient spot (such as the top or bottom of the screen).
3. Select the button and go to the **On Select** property.
4. Use the **Navigate** function to link it to another screen:

```
Navigate(Screen2, ScreenTransition.Fade)
```

1. This will move the user to **Screen2** with a fade effect.
2. Repeat for other screens to ensure smooth transitions.

Step 2: Creating a Home Button for Easy Access

If your app has multiple screens, users should always have a way to return to the **home screen.**

1. Insert a **new button** and place it in the header or footer.
2. Change its text to **"Home."**
3. Set its **On Select** property to:

```
Navigate(HomeScreen, ScreenTransition.None)
```

Now, users can always return to the main menu with one click.

Step 3: Using Icons for Better Navigation

Instead of text buttons, you can use icons for a **cleaner and modern look.**

1. Click **"Insert"** and select **"Icons."**
2. Choose symbols like **arrows, home, or back.**
3. Set their **On Select** properties to navigate between screens.

Icons make navigation more **intuitive and visually appealing.**

Best Practices for Layout and Navigation

To create a **user-friendly app**, follow these essential guidelines:

- **Keep the layout simple:** Avoid clutter; too many elements on one screen can confuse users.
- **Use clear labels:** Buttons and navigation links should be easy to understand.
- **Ensure consistency:** Place navigation buttons in the **same location** across all screens.
- **Add a back button:** Always provide an option to **return to the previous screen** to prevent frustration.
- **Test navigation flow:** Before publishing, **try navigating the app** as a user to ensure smooth transitions.

4.5 Using Formulas and Functions in Canvas Apps

Formulas and functions are the **backbone** of any powerful **Canvas App.** They allow you to automate actions, process data, and create an interactive experience for users. Without formulas, your app would be static, unable to respond to user inputs or perform calculations.

This section will guide you through **understanding and using formulas and functions** in a way that makes your app smarter and more efficient.

What Are Formulas and Functions?

A **formula** is a set of instructions that tells your app what to do. It works like a **mathematical equation** or a set of commands that respond to user actions.

A **function** is a predefined formula built into Power Apps that performs a specific task, like **calculations, navigation, filtering data, or updating records.**

Why Are Formulas Important?

- They allow your app to **respond to user input.**
- They help in **automating repetitive tasks.**
- They improve the app's **functionality and efficiency.**
- They make the app **interactive and dynamic.**

Step-by-Step Guide to Using Formulas and Functions

To use formulas effectively, you need to understand **where to write them and how they work.**

Step 1: Understanding the Formula Bar

In **Power Apps Studio**, every control (like buttons, labels, and input fields) has properties. The **Formula Bar** is where you enter the logic that makes these controls function dynamically.

1. **Select an object** (like a button or label).
2. **Go to the properties pane** (on the right).
3. **Find the Formula Bar** at the top.
4. **Enter your formula** based on what you want the control to do.

For example, if you want a button to navigate to another screen when clicked, enter this formula in the **On Select** property:

```
Navigate(Screen2, ScreenTransition.Fade)
```

This tells the app: *When the user clicks this button, move to Screen2 with a fade transition.*

Step 2: Using Functions for Common Tasks

Power Apps has **many built-in functions** that help in handling data, controlling navigation, and performing calculations.

Here are some of the most useful ones:

1. Displaying Data Dynamically

If you want to display a user's name from a database in a label, use this formula:

```
User().FullName
```

This will automatically show the logged-in user's full name on the

100

screen.

2. Performing Basic Calculations

Need to add two numbers from text input fields? Use:

```
TextInput1.Text + TextInput2.Text
```

This formula adds the values entered in **TextInput1** and **TextInput2** and displays the result.

3. Filtering Data in a Gallery

To display only **specific records** in a gallery, use the **Filter function**.

Example: If you have a list of employees and want to show only those in the "Sales" department:

```
Filter(EmployeeList, Department = "Sales")
```

This will display only employees from the **Sales** department.

4. Updating a Data Source

If you need to update a record in a **database**, use the **Patch function**.

Example: If a user edits their profile information and clicks a "Save" button, you can update their record like this:

```
Patch(EmployeeList, LookUp(EmployeeList, ID =
TextInputID.Text), {Name: TextInputName.Text, Email:
TextInputEmail.Text})
```

This formula **searches for the user by ID** and updates their name and email with new values.

5. Navigating Between Screens

To create smooth transitions between screens, use the **Navigate function**.

Example: If you want a button to take users back to the home screen:

```
Navigate(HomeScreen, ScreenTransition.Cover)
```

Step 3: Testing and Debugging Formulas

Writing formulas is **only half the process**—you also need to make sure they work correctly.

1. **Use the Formula Checker**

- When writing a formula, look for **red underlines** indicating an error.
- Click the **error message** to see what's wrong.

1. **Test Each Function**

- Run the app and **try different inputs** to ensure it works as expected.
- If something isn't working, check if you referenced the correct **controls and data sources.**

1. **Use the Monitor Tool**

- Power Apps provides a **Monitor Tool** to track how formulas are being executed.
- Open the Monitor and run your app to **see detailed logs** of how formulas are processed.

Best Practices for Writing Formulas in Canvas Apps

To ensure your formulas are **efficient and easy to maintain**, follow these best practices:

- **Keep formulas short and clear** – Break long formulas into smaller parts using variables.
- **Use meaningful names** – Instead of "TextInput1," rename it to "UserNameInput" for clarity.
- **Avoid hardcoding values** – Use dynamic data references instead of fixed text values.
- **Test as you go** – Don't wait until the end to check if your formulas work.
- **Use comments** – Add notes in complex formulas so others (or you in the future) understand them.

Example of a **commented formula**:

```
// Navigate to Home Screen with a transition
Navigate(HomeScreen, ScreenTransition.Fade)
```

Comments **help in debugging** and make formulas easier to understand.

Chapter 5: Model-Driven Apps

5.1 Overview of Model-Driven Apps

Model-Driven Apps are a **powerful way to build business applications** that follow a structured approach. Unlike Canvas Apps, where you design every element manually, Model-Driven Apps rely on **data models and relationships** to automatically create an efficient, well organized user experience.

These apps are ideal when working with **complex data, workflows, and business processes** that require consistency and structure. They provide a **guided, pre-built framework** that saves time while ensuring reliability.

Why Choose Model-Driven Apps?

Model-Driven Apps offer a **smart and efficient way to develop applications** by focusing on **data structure first** rather than manual design. Here's why they are beneficial:

- **Built for complex data** – Ideal for managing structured information and workflows.
- **Pre-configured layouts** – The system automatically arranges forms, views, and dashboards.
- **Seamless integration** – Works perfectly with Microsoft Dataverse and other data sources.
- **Security and control** – Offers built-in role-based security to protect sensitive data.
- **Scalability** – Grows with your business needs without requiring constant redesigning.

If your application **relies heavily on structured data, automation, and workflow management**, Model-Driven Apps provide a **fast and reliable solution**.

How Model-Driven Apps Work

Model-Driven Apps are built on a **data-first approach**, meaning that the app's structure depends on the underlying database and data relationships. Here's how they function:

1. **Data Structure** – The app is based on **tables, relationships, and business logic** stored in Microsoft Dataverse.
2. **User Interface** – The system automatically generates forms, views, and dashboards based on the data model.

3. **Business Logic and Automation** – Workflows, rules, and process automation make the app efficient.
4. **Security and Access Control** – Role-based security ensures users only see relevant data.

Since the system handles most of the **layout and functionality**, developers can focus on **business logic and data relationships** rather than spending time designing every screen manually.

Key Components of Model-Driven Apps

To build a successful Model-Driven App, you need to understand its core components:

1. Dataverse (Data Source)

Dataverse acts as the **foundation** of Model-Driven Apps. It stores structured data in tables (formerly called entities) that include:

- Standard tables (like accounts, contacts, or orders)
- Custom tables (created based on specific business needs)

2. Forms

Forms allow users to **view, edit, and enter data**. Different forms can be created for various user roles, ensuring the right people see the right information.

3. Views

Views define **how data is displayed** within the app. They can be customized to show **lists, charts, or detailed records** in an organized manner.

4. Dashboards

Dashboards provide an **interactive summary of data**, using charts, graphs, and key performance indicators (KPIs) to give users a quick overview of important metrics.

5. Business Rules and Workflows

Automation features like **business rules, workflows, and Power Automate** ensure tasks are streamlined, reducing manual effort and errors.

6. Security Roles

Role-based security settings ensure that each user **only has access to the data and features relevant to their role**, keeping sensitive information protected.

Step-by-Step Guide to Creating a Model-Driven App

Step 1: Access Power Apps Studio

1. Sign in to **Power Apps Studio** using your Microsoft account.
2. Click on **"Create"** and select **Model-Driven App** as your app type.

Step 2: Define the Data Structure

1. Choose **Microsoft Dataverse** as your data source.
2. Create **tables** (formerly entities) based on the data you need to manage.
3. Define **relationships** between tables (e.g., linking customers to orders).

Step 3: Design the User Interface

1. Set up **forms** for data entry.
2. Customize **views** to display records in a meaningful way.
3. Add **dashboards** to provide insights through charts and graphs.

Step 4: Apply Business Logic and Automation

1. Create **business rules** to enforce validation (e.g., requiring a customer name).
2. Set up **workflows** using Power Automate to automate approvals and notifications.

Step 5: Configure Security and Permissions

1. Assign **roles** to users (e.g., admin, manager, employee).
2. Control **data access** based on roles to protect sensitive information.

Step 6: Test and Publish the App

1. Preview the app to ensure all features work correctly.
2. Make adjustments if needed and publish the app for users to access.

Best Practices for Model-Driven Apps

To build an app that is **efficient, user-friendly, and scalable**, follow these best practices:

- **Plan the data model first** – A strong foundation ensures long-term efficiency.
- **Use meaningful table names** – Clear naming makes it easier to manage and update data.
- **Keep views and forms simple** – Overcomplicated layouts can confuse users.
- **Apply security roles carefully** – Protect sensitive data by granting access only where needed.
- **Test automation workflows** – Ensure business logic runs smoothly without errors.

5.2 Designing and Creating Model-Driven Apps

Model-Driven Apps provide a **structured and automated way** to develop applications that rely on well-organized data and business logic. Unlike Canvas Apps, where you have complete control over the design, Model-Driven Apps **generate layouts automatically** based

109

on the underlying data model. This makes them ideal for **managing complex business processes, workflows, and structured data**.

Creating a Model-Driven App requires **thoughtful planning and execution** to ensure that users get a smooth experience while interacting with the system. From defining the data structure to configuring user permissions, every step plays a crucial role in the app's effectiveness.

Understanding the Model-Driven App Design Approach

Before jumping into the development process, it's essential to understand the **core principles** behind Model-Driven Apps:

1. **Data is the foundation** – Unlike Canvas Apps, where design comes first, Model-Driven Apps focus on structuring data properly before the interface is built.
2. **Automatic UI generation** – Forms, views, and dashboards are created automatically based on the data model, ensuring consistency across the application.
3. **Integration with Dataverse** – These apps work seamlessly with Microsoft Dataverse, a **secure and scalable** data storage solution.
4. **Workflow automation** – Business logic and automation streamline processes, reducing the need for manual intervention.
5. **Security and role-based access** – Permissions control who can view, edit, or manage data, ensuring the right people have access to the right information.

By following these principles, you can create **efficient, scalable, and user-friendly applications** that enhance business operations.

Step-by-Step Guide to Designing and Creating a Model-Driven App

Building a Model-Driven App is a **systematic process** that involves planning the data structure, configuring user interfaces, and adding business rules. Below is a step-by-step approach to help you design and develop a functional app.

Step 1: Access Power Apps and Start a New Model-Driven App

1. **Log in to Power Apps Studio** using your Microsoft account.
2. Click on **"Create"** and choose **Model-Driven App** from the available options.
3. Select **"Blank app"** to start from scratch or use a template to speed up the process.
4. Give your app a **meaningful name** that reflects its purpose.

Step 2: Define the Data Structure in Dataverse

Since Model-Driven Apps rely on data, setting up a **well-structured database** is crucial:

1. **Go to Dataverse** in Power Apps and create a new **table** (previously known as an entity).
2. Define **columns (fields)** such as text, numbers, dates, or lookup fields that establish relationships between tables.
3. Establish **relationships** between different tables (e.g., linking customers to orders).
4. Customize the table settings to enforce **business rules, validation, and permissions**.

111

A well-structured data model ensures that the app functions smoothly and **delivers accurate, real-time information** to users.

Step 3: Design the App's User Interface

Once the data structure is in place, the next step is to configure the app's interface:

1. **Forms** – Create and customize forms that users will use to enter and edit data.
2. **Views** – Define how records will be displayed in lists or tables for easy navigation.
3. **Dashboards** – Design interactive dashboards that provide **visual insights** using charts and graphs.
4. **Navigation** – Organize the app layout to ensure a smooth user experience.

Since Model-Driven Apps automatically generate UI components, your main task is to **customize** them based on business needs.

Step 4: Implement Business Logic and Automation

To enhance functionality and reduce manual work, you need to add business rules and workflows:

1. **Business Rules** – Set conditions and actions to **automate validations and calculations**.
2. **Power Automate Flows** – Create workflows that trigger actions based on specific conditions (e.g., sending emails when a new record is created).
3. **Workflows and Processes** – Automate complex tasks,

approvals, and notifications to **improve efficiency**.

By integrating automation, the app **reduces errors, enhances productivity, and ensures consistency** in operations.

Step 5: Configure Security and User Access

Protecting data is crucial, especially when dealing with sensitive business information. Model-Driven Apps provide **role-based security**, allowing you to **control user access** at different levels:

1. **Assign security roles** to determine who can view, edit, or manage records.
2. **Restrict access** to sensitive data by defining **user permissions**.
3. **Use field-level security** to hide or lock specific fields for certain users.

This ensures that each user interacts with the app based on their **role and responsibilities**, keeping data secure and well-organized.

Step 6: Test the App and Gather Feedback

Before launching the app, **thorough testing** is essential to identify and resolve any issues:

1. Use **Test Mode** in Power Apps to check how the app functions.
2. Verify that **data entry, navigation, and automation work correctly**.
3. Ask **test users** to try the app and provide feedback on usability and performance.
4. Make necessary improvements based on feedback before

Publishing the app.

Step /: Publish and Share the App

Once testing is complete, you can **deploy the app** and make it available to users:

1. Click on **"Publish"** to finalize the app.
2. Share the app with **specific users or teams** based on role-based permissions.
3. Monitor app usage and **make updates** as needed to enhance functionality.

With a properly **designed and structured** Model-Driven App, businesses can **streamline operations, improve efficiency, and enhance decision-making**.

5.3 Working with Views, Forms, and Dashboards

Model-Driven Apps offer a **powerful way to organize, manage, and present data** in a structured format. Three essential components—**Views, Forms, and Dashboards**—help users interact with the app effectively. Each of these elements plays a crucial role in delivering a seamless experience, ensuring that users can **view, edit, and analyze data** with ease.

Mastering these features not only improves productivity but also enhances the overall functionality of the app. Whether it's a salesperson tracking leads, a manager reviewing reports, or an employee updating records, **Views, Forms, and Dashboards**

ensure data is

accessible, organized, and visually engaging.

Understanding Views, Forms, and Dashboards

Before diving into the creation and customization of these elements, let's explore what they are and why they matter.

1. Views – Organizing Data for Easy Access

Views are like **filtered lists** that allow users to see records in an organized manner. They define **how data appears in tables**, making it easy to search, sort, and filter information.

For example, if you're managing customer information, a View might show a list of **active customers**, displaying relevant details such as names, emails, and recent interactions.

Types of Views

- **Public Views** – Available to all users within the app.
- **Personal Views** – Created by individual users for their own use.
- **System Views** – Predefined by administrators and cannot be modified by general users.

2. Forms – Editing and Managing Data

Forms provide **a structured way to input, edit, and view records**. When a user selects a record from a View, the Form opens, displaying **detailed information** about that record.

Forms ensure that data entry is **consistent and user-friendly**. Instead of working with raw tables, users interact with a well-organized layout, making data management more efficient.

Types of Forms

- **Main Forms** – The primary form for creating and editing records.
- **Quick View Forms** – Displays related record information without opening a new page.
- **Quick Create Forms** – Allows users to add new records with minimal steps.

3. Dashboards – Visualizing Data for Better Decisions

Dashboards bring data **to life** by presenting key insights through **charts, graphs, and summaries**. Instead of manually sifting through records, users can see an **overview of important metrics** at a glance. For example, a sales team might use a Dashboard to track **monthly revenue, customer engagement, and pending deals**. These visual elements help users **identify trends, monitor performance, and make informed decisions**.

Types of Dashboards

- **Personal Dashboards** – Created by individual users for their needs.
- **System Dashboards** – Designed for organization-wide use, offering a standardized view.

Step-by-Step Guide to Creating and Customizing Views, Forms, and Dashboards

Now that we understand the importance of these elements, let's explore how to create and customize them effectively.

Step 1: Creating and Customizing Views

1. **Go to Power Apps Studio** and navigate to Dataverse.
2. Select the table you want to create a View for.
3. Click on the **"Views"** tab and choose **"Create New View."**
4. **Select the columns** you want to display, such as names, dates, or statuses.
5. **Apply filters and sorting options** to refine how records appear.
6. Save and publish the View to make it accessible.

Customization Tip: Use **conditional formatting** to highlight important data, such as overdue tasks or high-priority requests.

Step 2: Designing and Configuring Forms

1. In Power Apps Studio, navigate to **Dataverse > Tables** and select the desired table.
2. Click on the **"Forms"** tab and choose **"Create New Form."**
3. Drag and drop fields to arrange the layout based on user needs.
4. Add **sections and tabs** to group related information.
5. Configure **business rules and automation** to validate inputs and trigger actions.
6. Save and publish the Form for users to access.

Customization Tip: Use **pre-filled fields and dropdowns** to minimize manual data entry and improve accuracy.

Step 3: Building Interactive Dashboards

1. Navigate to **Power Apps > Dashboards** and select **"Create New Dashboard."**
2. Choose a **layout template** based on how you want to display data.
3. Add components such as **charts, tables, and lists** to visualize key metrics.
4. Configure filters to allow users to **drill down into specific data points**.
5. Save and publish the Dashboard, making it available to the appropriate users.

Customization Tip: Incorporate **real-time data updates** to ensure users always have the latest insights.

5.4 Setting Up Business Rules and Processes

A well-structured system **doesn't just store data—it ensures that everything runs smoothly and efficiently**. Business rules and processes are the backbone of any well-functioning Model-Driven App, **helping to automate workflows, maintain data accuracy, and enforce consistency across the system**.

Without these rules in place, mistakes can slip through, **data entry errors become common, and users may struggle to follow standard procedures**. Setting up business rules and processes ensures that **each step is followed correctly**, guiding users while reducing manual work.

Understanding Business Rules and Processes

What Are Business Rules?

Business rules are **logic-based conditions** that help control how data behaves in your app. They allow you to **set requirements, show or hide fields, validate inputs, and trigger actions—all without needing complex coding**.

For example, in a sales app, you might create a rule that **prevents a deal from being marked as "Closed" unless a contract is attached**. This **ensures that all steps are completed before moving forward**.

What Are Business Processes?

Business processes guide users **through structured workflows**, ensuring that tasks are completed in the right order. A well-designed business process:

- **Leads users step by step,** making complex tasks easier.
- **Ensures consistency,** so employees follow the same procedures every time.
- **Reduces errors** by automating repetitive tasks.

For example, in a customer service app, a business process might ensure that **every complaint is logged, assigned to an agent, and resolved within a set time frame**.

Step-by-Step Guide to Setting Up Business Rules

Business rules help keep data organized and prevent users from making mistakes. Follow these steps to create and apply business rules in your Model-Driven App:

Step 1: Access the Business Rules Designer

1. Open **Power Apps** and go to the **Dataverse section**.
2. Select the table where you want to apply the business rule.
3. Click on **"Business Rules"** and choose **"New Business Rule."**

Step 2: Define the Conditions

1. In the Business Rules Designer, drag and drop a **"Condition"** onto the canvas.
2. Set the **criteria** that must be met.

- Example: If the "Payment Status" field is empty, trigger a warning.

1. Click **"Apply"** to save the condition.

Step 3: Add Actions to the Rule

Once a condition is set, define what should happen when the condition is met:

- **Show error messages** – Prevent users from submitting incomplete or incorrect data.
- **Set field values** – Automatically fill in a field based on another input.

121

- **Enable or disable fields** – Restrict editing when certain conditions apply.
- **Hide or show fields** – Display only relevant information based on user actions.

For example, if a customer selects "Other" as their payment method, a new field can appear asking for additional details.

Step 4: Save and Activate the Rule

1. Click **"Save"** once all actions are defined.
2. Select **"Activate"** to apply the rule to your app.
3. Test the rule by entering sample data to confirm it works as expected.

Creating Business Process Flows (BPFs)

Business Process Flows (BPFs) **guide users through a series of steps to complete a task efficiently**. Follow these steps to create one:

Step 1: Open the Process Designer

1. In Power Apps, go to **Dataverse > Processes**.
2. Click **"New"** and select **"Business Process Flow."**
3. Name your process and select the table it applies to.

Step 2: Define Stages and Steps

1. A BPF consists of **stages** (major steps in a process).
2. Each stage has **steps** (individual tasks required to complete that stage).

3. Drag a new **stage** onto the canvas and name it based on the process flow.
4. Inside each stage, define the **required fields** that must be completed before moving to the next step.

For example, a hiring process might have these stages:

- **Application Review** (Fields: Candidate Name, Resume, Job Position)
- **Interview** (Fields: Interview Date, Feedback, Next Steps)
- **Offer Approval** (Fields: Salary, Start Date, Offer Letter)

Step 3: Set Conditions and Actions

- Use **conditions** to move users through different paths based on their inputs.
- Add **automations** to trigger actions, such as sending email notifications when a stage is completed.

Step 4: Save, Activate, and Test the Process

1. Click **"Save"** and then **"Activate"** to apply the process to your app.
2. Test the flow by **creating sample records** and moving through the stages to ensure everything works correctly.

5.5 Tips for Model-Driven Apps

Model-Driven Apps are designed to **simplify complex business processes** by structuring data, automating tasks, and providing users with an intuitive experience. However, to create an app that is truly efficient and user-friendly, **proper planning and thoughtful design are essential**.

Many developers and businesses make the mistake of jumping straight into development without considering **how users will interact with the app, what data is necessary, and how processes should flow**. By following best practices, **you can avoid frustration, reduce errors, and build an app that meets real-world needs effectively**.

Here are essential tips to ensure your Model-Driven App is well structured, scalable, and easy to use.

1. Start with a Clear Plan

Before building your app, take the time to map out its purpose. **Ask yourself these key questions:**

- What problem is the app solving?
- Who will use it, and what tasks will they perform?
- What data is required, and how should it be structured?
- What workflows and automations will improve efficiency?

Creating a blueprint of your app's structure ensures that **you don't waste time on unnecessary features or overlook critical elements**.

2. Keep the User Experience Simple

A great app should be **easy to navigate and require minimal training**. Overcomplicating layouts, adding too many forms, or cluttering dashboards with unnecessary details can frustrate users.

Best practices for an intuitive experience:

- **Limit the number of clicks needed to complete an action.** Users should be able to perform tasks with minimal effort.
- **Use clear labels and tooltips.** Ambiguous names can confuse users, so make sure each field and button is clearly labeled.
- **Prioritize important information.** Place essential data at the top of forms and dashboards for quick access.

An app that feels effortless to use **increases productivity and reduces errors**.

3. Optimize Performance and Speed

A slow or unresponsive app can disrupt workflow and create frustration. **To ensure fast performance:**

- **Avoid excessive fields and complex calculations** on a single form.
- **Use filters and search functions** to load only the necessary data.
- **Regularly test and monitor performance** to identify areas that need improvement.

Efficiency matters, especially for apps that handle large amounts of data. Keeping your app optimized ensures a **smooth experience for**

all users.

4. Use Business Rules to Automate Manual Tasks

Manually entering data, correcting mistakes, and guiding users through processes can be time-consuming. **Business rules help automate these actions, reducing human error and improving accuracy.**

Effective ways to use business rules:

- **Automatically fill in fields** based on user inputs.
- **Set validation rules** to prevent incorrect data entry.
- **Show or hide fields dynamically** to simplify forms and keep them relevant.

Automation not only makes tasks easier but also **ensures consistency and compliance with company policies**.

5. Customize Views and Dashboards for Clarity

Users rely on views and dashboards to quickly access **relevant information**. A poorly designed interface can make it difficult to find important data.

Tips for effective views and dashboards:

- **Create different views for different roles.** Not all users need access to the same data—customizing views ensures each user sees only what they need.
- **Use charts and graphs** to present complex data visually.

- **Group related data together** so users don't have to switch between multiple screens.

A well-designed dashboard **makes data analysis easier and decision-making faster**.

6. Test Before Deployment

Many issues in apps come from skipping the **testing phase**. Before rolling out your Model-Driven App, **test it under different scenarios** to catch potential problems.

What to check during testing:

- Are all business rules working as expected?
- Do forms, views, and dashboards display correctly on different devices?
- Are workflows and automation triggering properly?
- Are users able to complete tasks without confusion?

Catching issues before deployment **prevents downtime, reduces frustration, and ensures a smooth launch**.

7. Keep Your App Updated and Scalable

As business needs change, your app should **adapt** to accommodate new workflows, user feedback, and system updates.

How to maintain a scalable app:

- **Regularly review user feedback** to improve usability.
- **Update business processes** as workflows evolve.
- **Ensure security settings are up to date** to protect sensitive data.
- **Train users on new features** to maximize adoption.

A Model-Driven App isn't something you build once and forget—it should **grow alongside your business, continuously improving over time**.

Chapter 6: Customizing and Enhancing Apps

⁓◯⦿◯⁓

6.1 Working with Custom Controls

Custom controls **bring a unique touch to an app**, allowing developers to create a more interactive, user-friendly experience. While standard controls serve many purposes, they often **lack the flexibility needed for specific business needs**. This is where custom controls step in—giving you the ability to **fine-tune every detail of your app's interface and functionality**.

Whether it's improving user input, enhancing visual appeal, or **introducing dynamic elements**, custom controls help **bridge the gap between default features and real-world requirements**.

Let's explore how to use custom controls effectively and create an **app experience that is both powerful and intuitive**.

Understanding Custom Controls

A **custom control** is a specialized UI element that enhances the way users interact with an app. Unlike standard controls such as text fields or dropdowns, custom controls **offer more flexibility** and can be tailored to specific needs.

For example, if your app requires a **more engaging way to input numerical values**, a **slider control** might be better than a simple text box. If users need to upload images, a **custom image uploader** could improve the experience by allowing previews before submission.

By using custom controls, you ensure that your app **functions smoothly, looks professional, and aligns with your business goals**.

How to Add Custom Controls to Your App

Integrating custom controls requires careful thought. Here's a **step by step** guide to help you add them seamlessly:

Step 1: Identify the Need for a Custom Control

Before creating or adding a custom control, ask yourself:

- What problem am I trying to solve?
- Can a built-in control achieve this, or do I need a custom solution?
- How will this improve the user experience?

For example, if users struggle with entering long descriptions, you might add a **rich text editor** instead of a plain text box to allow better formatting.

Step 2: Choose the Right Control

Selecting the appropriate control is crucial. Some commonly used custom controls include:

- **Slider Controls** – Ideal for adjusting values dynamically (e.g., price filters).
- **Toggle Switches** – A modern alternative to checkboxes for on/off functions.
- **Signature Panels** – Useful for capturing electronic signatures.
- **Multi-Select Dropdowns** – Allows users to select multiple items at once.

Each control should **enhance usability and improve efficiency,** rather than complicating the interface.

Step 3: Add and Configure the Custom Control

Once you've selected the right control, follow these steps to add it to your app:

1. **Open the App Designer**

- Navigate to the screen where you want to place the control.

1. **Insert the Control**

- Select the "Insert" option and choose the control type.

1. **Customize the Properties**

- Adjust settings such as size, color, font, and behavior to match your app's theme.

1. **Connect Data (If Needed)**

- Link the control to a data source for dynamic content (e.g., a dropdown that pulls categories from a database).

1. **Test the Control**

- Ensure it functions correctly across different devices before finalizing.

Step 4: Test and Optimize Performance

After adding the custom control, thorough testing is essential. **A well-designed control should feel natural to users and respond instantly**.

Key areas to check:

- Does the control work smoothly without delays?
- Is it responsive across different screen sizes?
- Does it integrate correctly with other features in the app?

If the control **feels sluggish or unresponsive**, optimize it by **reducing unnecessary scripts, simplifying animations, or adjusting settings**.

6.2 Using Power Apps Component Framework (PCF)

Creating an app that truly meets user needs often requires **more than just basic features**. Sometimes, you need deeper customization to enhance both functionality and design. This is where the **Power Apps Component Framework (PCF)** becomes invaluable. It allows developers to **go beyond default controls**, bringing a richer, more interactive experience to applications.

With PCF, you can build **custom components** that seamlessly integrate with your app, improving how users interact with data and visuals. Whether you want to create **dynamic charts, interactive maps, or advanced input fields**, PCF gives you the **freedom to shape the app the way you envision it**.

What is Power Apps Component Framework (PCF)?

PCF is a tool that allows developers to **build and use custom components** inside Power Apps. Unlike standard controls, which come with limited functionality, PCF components **let you define how data is displayed and interacted with**.

For instance, if you want an **animated progress bar** instead of a static percentage field, PCF makes it possible. If a business needs a **custom date picker** that integrates with external data sources, PCF provides that flexibility.

By using PCF, you ensure that your app **isn't just functional but also visually appealing and highly user-friendly**.

How to Use Power Apps Component Framework (PCF)

To get started with PCF, follow these steps carefully:

Step 1: Set Up the Development Environment

Before building a custom component, you need to **set up the right tools**.

1. **Install Node.js**

- PCF relies on **Node.js** for running scripts and managing dependencies.

1. **Set Up Power Apps CLI (Command-Line Interface)**

- The Power Apps CLI allows you to create, test, and deploy PCF components.

1. **Install Visual Studio Code**

- A code editor like **Visual Studio Code** makes it easier to write and manage PCF projects.

1. **Verify the Setup**

- Run a test command in the terminal to check if everything is installed correctly.

Step 2: Create a New PCF Component

Now that the environment is ready, it's time to build a custom component.

1. **Open the Command Line and Navigate to Your Workspace**

- Choose a folder where your project files will be stored.

1. **Run the PCF Initialization Command**

- Use the following command to create a new component:

```
pac pcf init --namespace MyCompany --name MyCustomComponent
--template field
```

- Replace MyCompany with your preferred namespace and MyCustomComponent with the component's name.

1. **Open the Project in Visual Studio Code**

- Navigate to the newly created folder and open it in **Visual Studio Code**.

Step 3: Develop the Component

Now, you need to define how the component looks and functions.

1. **Edit the Control Manifest.xml File**

134

- This file describes how the component behaves, including input properties, output events, and styling.

1. **Write the Component Logic**

- Open the **index.ts** file and add JavaScript or Typescript code to define the component's behavior.

1. **Apply Custom Styles**

- Modify the **CSS file** to match the app's theme and design.

Step 4: Test the Component

Before deploying the component, it's essential to test it for errors and functionality.

1. **Run the Local Test Environment**

- Use this command to see how your component works:

```
npm start
```

- The browser will open a preview of your component.

1. **Fix Any Issues**

- Check for errors, ensure the component is responsive, and refine any glitches.

Step 5: Deploy the PCF Component to Power Apps

Once testing is complete, the next step is to **package and deploy the component** to Power Apps.

1. **Build the Component**

- Run this command to generate the required files:

```
npm run build
```

1. **Add the Component to Power Apps**

- Navigate to **Power Apps**, open your app, and **import the PCF component** from the solutions menu.

1. **Use the Component in Your App**

- Drag and drop the custom component onto the canvas and **configure its settings**.

6.3 Incorporating Custom Connectors

When building apps, one of the biggest challenges is ensuring smooth communication between different services and data sources. **Custom connectors** help solve this problem by allowing Power Apps to connect with external applications, databases, and APIs that aren't natively supported.

Instead of being limited to the built-in connectors provided by Power Apps, you can **create your own custom connector** to link your app with any third-party service. Whether you need to retrieve data from a company database, integrate with a specialized tool, or pull real-time information from an external system, custom connectors give you the power to do so.

What Are Custom Connectors?

Custom connectors act as **a bridge between Power Apps and external services**. They define how your app communicates with another system, specifying the requests it can send and the data it can receive.

For example, if your business uses an internal **customer management system**, but it doesn't have a built-in Power Apps connector, you can create a custom connector to fetch **customer details, transaction history, or order statuses** directly into your app.

This approach ensures that your app remains **well-connected, efficient, and capable of handling real-world business needs**.

How to Create and Use Custom Connectors

To make full use of custom connectors, follow these detailed steps:

Step 1: Set Up the API

Before creating a connector, ensure that the external service you want to connect to has a **working API**.

1. **Find the API Documentation**

- Check if the service provides an API. Look for details like authentication requirements, available endpoints, and response formats.

1. **Test the API Using Postman**

- Tools like **Postman** help you understand how the API works before integrating it into Power Apps.
- Send test requests to ensure the API is responsive and returns the correct data.

Step 2: Create a Custom Connector in Power Apps

Once the API is ready, the next step is to build the custom connector.

1. **Open Power Apps and Navigate to Custom Connectors**

- Go to the **Power Apps portal** and click on **Custom Connectors** under the **Data** section.

1. **Click "New Custom Connector" and Choose "From Blank"**

- This option allows you to define a completely new connector from scratch.

1. **Provide Basic Information**

- Give your connector a **name** and a **description** that explains its purpose.

1. **Enter the API Details**

- Add the **base URL** of the API you are connecting to.
- Specify the **authentication method** (e.g., API key, OAuth, or basic authentication).

Step 3: Define the Connector's Actions

Now, it's time to set up the requests your connector will handle.

1. **Add a New Action**

- Click **"New Action"** and enter details for the API request.

1. **Specify the Request Type**

- Choose the correct method:
- **GET** – Retrieve data from the external service.
- **POST** – Send data to the external service.
- **PUT** – Update existing data.
- **DELETE** – Remove data.

1. **Configure Request Parameters**

- If the API requires inputs (like an ID or search term), define them here.

1. **Define the Response Format**

- Power Apps needs to know how the API's response looks. Use a **sample response** from Postman or the API documentation to guide this step.

Step 4: Test the Custom Connector

Before using it in an app, verify that the connector works correctly.

1. **Click "Test" in the Power Apps Connector Editor**

- Run a test request and check if the expected response appears.

1. **Fix Any Errors**

- If the request fails, check the API documentation and adjust your connector settings as needed.

Step 5: Use the Custom Connector in Power Apps

Now that the connector is working, you can **integrate it into your app**.

1. **Open Your App in Power Apps Studio**

- Go to the app where you want to use the connector.

1. **Add the Custom Connector**

- Click on **"Data"**, then **"Add Data"**, and select your newly created connector.

1. Use the Connector in a Formula

- Call the connector in Power Apps using a formula like this:

```
CustomConnectorName.FunctionName(Parameter)
```

- Replace FunctionName with the specific API request you created.

1. Bind the Data to Your UI

- Connect the response data to labels, tables, or other components to display the retrieved information.

6.4 Integrating External APIs and Data Sources

In the digital age, applications thrive on data. Whether it's retrieving customer details, tracking orders, or pulling in live updates from an external system, the ability to **connect to different data sources** is what makes an app truly powerful. Power Apps makes this possible by allowing seamless **integration with external APIs and data sources**, ensuring that your applications stay dynamic and responsive to real time information.

If you want to enhance your app's capabilities and provide users with up-to-date data, learning how to **connect external APIs and data sources** is essential. Let's dive into the step-by-step process of integrating external services into Power Apps.

Why Integrate External APIs and Data Sources?

Not all data resides within Power Apps. Businesses often use **various platforms** like databases, cloud storage, CRMs, and financial systems. APIs (Application Programming Interfaces) allow these systems to **communicate with Power Apps**, ensuring that important information is easily accessible.

For example, if your company manages customer records in an **online CRM**, an API connection can bring that data into Power Apps, so employees **don't have to switch between multiple platforms**. Instead, everything they need is available in one place, making work **more efficient and streamlined**.

How to Integrate External APIs and Data Sources in Power Apps

Connecting external data sources might sound complex, but with the right approach, it becomes a straightforward process. Follow these steps to **integrate external APIs and bring external data into Power Apps**.

Step 1: Identify the External API or Data Source

Before setting up the connection, determine where the data will come from.

1. **Check if Power Apps Has a Built-in Connector**

- Power Apps offers **pre-built connectors** for services like Share-

142

Point, SQL Server, Salesforce, and more.

- If a built-in connector exists, use it for an easier integration.

1. **If No Built-in Connector Exists, Use a Custom API**

- When dealing with unique services, you will need to connect through a **custom API**.
- Look for API documentation to understand how the system allows data access.

Step 2: Obtain API Access and Credentials

Most APIs require authentication before granting access to data.

1. **Check API Authentication Requirements**

- APIs may use different methods for security, such as:
- API Keys
- OAuth 2.0
- Basic Authentication (Username & Password)

1. **Generate API Credentials**

- If an API key is required, generate one from the service's developer portal.
- If OAuth is needed, register an app in the external service and obtain a **Client ID and Secret**.

Step 3: Connect Power Apps to the External API

Once authentication is set up, integrate the API into Power Apps.

1. **Use a Pre-built Connector (If Available)**

- Open **Power Apps Studio** and go to **Data > Add Data**.
- Search for the service you need and **select the connector**.
- Log in with your credentials to authorize the connection.

1. **Create a Custom Connector (If No Pre-built Option Exists)**

- If a built-in connector isn't available, you will need to **set up a custom connector** (as explained in the previous section).
- Navigate to **Custom Connectors** and create a new one by specifying the API endpoint and authentication details.

Step 4: Retrieve Data from the External Source

After connecting the API, bring data into your app.

1. **Use the API in a Formula**

- If using a custom connector, retrieve data with a formula like this:

```
CustomConnectorName.GetData(Parameter)
```

- This pulls data from the external system into Power Apps.

1. **Display the Data in Your App**

*   Connect the response to **labels, tables, or dropdown menus** to show the information in a user-friendly way.

Step 5: Send Data to the External API (Optional)

In some cases, you may need to **send information back to the external system**.

1. **Use API Methods Like POST or PUT**

*   To send data, use a formula like:

```
CustomConnectorName.SubmitData(Value)
```

*   This ensures Power Apps can update records in the external service.

1. **Confirm Data Syncing**

*   Always verify that the data successfully updates in the external system.

Tips for Integrating External APIs

To make the integration process smooth and efficient, follow these **best practices**:

- **Ensure API Security** – Use **secure authentication** methods to prevent unauthorized access.
- **Minimize API Calls** – Too many requests can **slow down** your app. Retrieve data only when needed.
- **Handle Errors Gracefully** – If an API request fails, **display user-friendly error messages** instead of raw system errors.
- **Keep Data Updated** – Use refresh functions to **load the latest data** when the app opens.
- **Test Thoroughly** – Before deploying, test the integration to ensure all functions work correctly.

Integrating external APIs and data sources unlocks **endless possibilities** for Power Apps, allowing your application to work **seamlessly with other platforms**. Whether you need to **pull customer information, track live inventory, or update sales records**, APIs help you connect and **create a unified system**.

By following the **right steps**, setting up authentication, and using **smart data retrieval techniques**, you can make your Power Apps **more powerful, efficient, and user-friendly.**

6.5 Creating Reusable Components for Apps

When building applications, efficiency is key. A well-designed app should not only function smoothly but also be **easy to maintain and scale**. One of the best ways to achieve this is by creating **reusable components**—elements that can be used in multiple places within the app without needing to be rebuilt from scratch.

Reusable components **save time, reduce errors, and improve consistency** across different sections of an application. Whether you're working on **buttons, navigation bars, input fields, or complex data tables**, having standardized components ensures a smoother development process and a more cohesive user experience.

Let's explore how to **design, create, and use reusable components** effectively in your apps.

1. Understanding Reusable Components

A reusable component is a **pre-designed element** that performs a specific function and can be used multiple times within an application. Instead of designing the same button, form, or navigation bar repeatedly, you create it **once** and use it wherever needed.

These components can be as simple as **a styled button** or as complex as **a data entry form** that interacts with multiple databases. The goal is to **build once, use many times**—ensuring that any updates or modifications to the component automatically apply wherever it is used.

For example, if your app requires **a custom input field for collecting user data**, you can design a reusable component that includes built-in validation, formatting, and styling. Instead of recreating the field every time, you simply **insert the component** wherever it is needed.

2. Benefits of Using Reusable Components

1. Saves Time and Effort

Instead of redesigning elements from scratch, you can use a **prebuilt component**, reducing development time and increasing efficiency.

2. Ensures Consistency

Using the same component across different screens maintains a **uniform look and behavior**, providing a seamless user experience.

3. Simplifies Maintenance

If you need to update a component, you only have to **modify it in one place**, and the changes automatically apply everywhere the component is used.

4. Reduces Errors

Since reusable components are **tested and optimized**, they minimize the chances of introducing errors when developing new features.

5. Enhances Scalability

As your application grows, reusability ensures that adding new features is **more efficient and manageable**.

3. Steps to Create Reusable Components in Power Apps

To build effective reusable components, follow these steps:

Step 1: Identify Common Elements

Start by analyzing your app and identifying elements that **appear frequently**. These could include:

- **Buttons with standard actions** (e.g., Save, Cancel, Submit)
- **Input fields with validation** (e.g., email or phone number fields)
- **Navigation menus**
- **Pop-up messages**
- **Data tables and lists**

Look for elements that **serve the same purpose** across multiple screens and group them into reusable components.

Step 2: Create a New Component

1. **Open Power Apps Studio** and navigate to the **Components** tab.
2. Click **New Component** to create a blank component.
3. Give it a meaningful name, such as **"Custom Button"** or **"User Input Field"** for easy identification.

Step 3: Design the Component

1. Add **controls** such as labels, text input fields, buttons, or icons based on your component's purpose.
2. Customize properties like color, font, size, and alignment to match your app's design.
3. Use **variables and input properties** to allow flexibility when the component is used in different parts of the app.

149

For example, if designing a **custom button**, allow users to **change the text and color dynamically** by adding input properties.

Step 4: Configure Behavior and Actions

1. Add event handlers for **clicks, text inputs, or hover effects** using Power Apps formulas.
2. Set up navigation links or data submission functions if required.
3. Test interactions to ensure they work correctly across different screens.

For instance, a reusable **form component** can be configured to **autofill data** or **validate inputs before submission**.

Step 5: Save and Use the Component

1. Once the component is fully designed and tested, save it.
2. Insert it into multiple screens by selecting **"Insert Component"** from the toolbar.
3. Adjust properties as needed to fit different scenarios without modifying the core design.

Step 6: Update and Maintain Components

Over time, you may need to improve or modify components. Instead of updating multiple instances manually, you can **edit the reusable component once**, and the changes will reflect throughout the app.

For example, if you decide to **change the color scheme** for buttons, updating the component will **automatically apply the new style** across all screens where it is used.

4. Best Practices for Reusable Components

1. Keep Components Modular

Each component should have a **single, clear purpose** to make it easy to reuse in different contexts.

2. Use Input Properties for Flexibility

Allow components to accept **dynamic values**, such as labels, colors, or actions, so they can be used in various situations without modification.

3. Avoid Hardcoded Values

Use **variables and parameters** instead of fixed values so that components can adapt to different use cases.

4. Test Components Thoroughly

Ensure each component works properly before using it in multiple places. Test different inputs, actions, and scenarios to avoid unexpected issues.

5. Document Component Usage

Provide **clear instructions** on how to use each component so that other developers or team members can easily implement them.

5. Real-World Example: Reusable Notification Banner

Let's say you need to **display important messages** across different parts of your app, such as error messages, success confirmations, or warnings. Instead of creating a separate banner for each screen, you can design a **single reusable notification component**.

Steps to Create a Notification Banner Component

1. **Create a new component** and name it **"Notification Banner"**.
2. Add a **rectangle shape** for the background and set its visibility to conditional logic.
3. Insert a **text label** to display messages dynamically.
4. Add an **input property** so messages can be customized based on the situation.
5. Use color coding:

- Green for success messages
- Red for errors
- Yellow for warnings

1. Save and **use it across multiple screens** by simply updating the text and color dynamically.

With this approach, whenever you need to notify users about an action, **you don't have to recreate the banner**—you just call the component and set its message.

Chapter 7: Automating Processes with Power Automate

7.1 Introduction to Power Automate

In every business, tasks are performed repeatedly. Whether it's sending email notifications, updating records, or processing approvals, these actions take up valuable time. Manually handling them can lead to delays, errors, and frustration. This is where **Power Automate** becomes a game-changer.

Power Automate is a **tool designed to automate repetitive tasks**, allowing businesses to work **faster, smarter, and more efficiently**. It helps you **reduce manual effort, improve accuracy, and ensure that workflows run seamlessly**—without the constant need for human intervention.

Think about a scenario where an employee submits a request for leave. Instead of **manually checking emails and forwarding approvals**, Power Automate can **automatically send notifications**

to managers, track responses, and update records—all without anyone lifting a finger.

What is Power Automate?

Power Automate is a **cloud-based service** that enables users to **build automated workflows between different apps and services**. These workflows, known as **flows**, can help businesses:

- **Automate repetitive tasks** like data entry, approvals, and notifications.
- **Connect different applications** such as Microsoft 365, SharePoint, Outlook, and third-party services.
- **Trigger actions based on specific events**, ensuring timely responses.
- **Eliminate human errors** by following a predefined set of actions.

With Power Automate, you don't need advanced technical knowledge. Its **user-friendly interface** allows anyone to build automation workflows using simple steps.

Benefits of Power Automate

Automating tasks with Power Automate brings a variety of benefits:

1. Saves Time and Effort

Manually handling repetitive tasks slows down work. Power Automate ensures that **processes run automatically**, freeing up employees to focus on more meaningful tasks.

2. Reduces Human Errors

Mistakes happen when tasks are performed manually. Automation follows a **structured process**, ensuring consistency and accuracy in every action.

3. Improves Productivity

By automating workflows, employees no longer have to spend hours on routine work. This increases efficiency and helps businesses achieve **more in less time**.

4. Enhances Collaboration

Power Automate connects different applications, allowing data to flow smoothly between systems. This ensures that **teams always have access to up-to-date information**.

5. Provides Real-Time Notifications

With automated alerts and reminders, users **stay informed about important updates, deadlines, and approvals**, ensuring smooth operations.

How Power Automate Works

Power Automate is built on a **simple concept**: workflows are triggered when certain conditions are met, and actions follow automatically.

Key Components of Power Automate

To understand how it functions, let's break it down into three main elements:

1. Triggers

A **trigger** is the event that **starts** an automation process. Examples include:

- A new email arrives in your inbox.
- A file is uploaded to a folder.
- A form is submitted.

2. Actions

Once a trigger occurs, Power Automate performs **actions** such as:

- Sending an email notification.
- Updating a database record.
- Posting a message in Teams.

3. Conditions

Conditions help determine what happens next. For example:

- If an expense is under $500, approve it automatically.
- If an order is delayed, send an alert to the customer service team.

By combining these elements, Power Automate can **handle complex processes efficiently**.

Step-by-Step Guide to Creating an Automated Workflow

Setting up a workflow in Power Automate is simple. Follow these steps to get started:

Step 1: Access Power Automate

1. Sign in to **Power Automate** through your Microsoft 365 account.
2. Click on **"Create"** to start building a new workflow.

Step 2: Choose a Trigger

1. Select **"Automated cloud flow"** for an event-based workflow.
2. Pick a trigger, such as **"When an email arrives"** or **"When a file is added to SharePoint"**.

Step 3: Add Actions

1. Click **"New Step"** to define what should happen after the trigger.
2. Choose from available actions like **sending an email, creating a task, or updating a database**.
3. Configure the action by specifying details like recipient email addresses, message content, or file locations.

Step 4: Apply Conditions (Optional)

1. If needed, add a condition to control the workflow logic.
2. For example, set a rule that **only sends an approval request if an expense exceeds $1000**.

Step 5: Test the Workflow

1. Click **"Save"** and then **"Test"** to run the automation.
2. Perform the trigger action (such as sending an email) to see if the workflow executes correctly.

Step 6: Activate the Flow

1. Once testing is successful, **turn on the workflow** to start automating your process.
2. Monitor activity and check logs to ensure smooth operation.

Examples of Power Automate in Action

1. Automating Approval Processes

A manager receives multiple leave requests daily. Instead of **manually approving each one**, Power Automate can:

- Send a request to the manager when an employee submits a form.
- Allow the manager to approve or reject the request with a single click.
- Automatically notify the employee of the decision.

2. Sending Automatic Reminders

Missed deadlines can disrupt business operations. Power Automate can:

- Track due dates for tasks.
- Send automatic reminders before deadlines.
- Notify responsible team members to ensure tasks are completed on time.

3. Syncing Data Between Apps

Keeping records up-to-date manually is challenging. Power Automate can:

- Sync customer data between Excel, SharePoint, and a CRM system.
- Ensure that changes made in one system are reflected in all others.
- Eliminate the need for double data entry.

7.2 Connecting Power Apps to Power Automate

Bringing automation into your applications is one of the most effective ways to improve efficiency, reduce manual work, and create a seamless user experience. By integrating **Power Apps** with **Power Automate**, you can design apps that don't just collect data but also trigger actions automatically.

Whether it's sending a notification, updating a database, or processing approvals, this connection ensures that everything runs smoothly without requiring users to switch between different tools.

Why Connect Power Apps to Power Automate?

Power Apps allows you to create custom applications, while Power Automate enables you to automate tasks and workflows. By combining both, you can:

- **Automate complex tasks** with a simple button press.
- **Enhance user experience** by eliminating manual steps.
- **Ensure real-time updates** without delays.
- **Reduce errors** by standardizing processes.

For example, instead of manually approving expense reports, you can build an app where employees submit requests, and with one tap, Power Automate sends notifications, updates records, and completes the approval process.

Understanding the Connection

When integrating Power Apps with Power Automate, you create **flows** that trigger actions based on events occurring in your app.

Key Components of the Integration:

- **Power Apps as a Trigger:** The user performs an action (e.g., pressing a button).
- **Power Automate as the Workflow Engine:** The flow is executed based on the trigger.
- **Actions that Follow:** The automated process updates records, sends emails, or performs other predefined tasks.

This connection transforms simple applications into powerful, action driven tools.

Step-by-Step Guide to Connecting Power Apps with Power Automate

Now, let's go through the process of linking Power Apps to Power Automate and building a workflow that performs a real-time action.

Step 1: Open Power Automate and Create a Flow

1. Sign in to **Power Automate** through your Microsoft account.
2. Click **"Create"** at the top of the screen.
3. Select **"Instant cloud flow"** (this allows manual triggers from Power Apps).
4. Name your flow appropriately, such as **"Send Email from Power Apps"**.

Step 2: Choose Power Apps as the Trigger

1. In the flow designer, search for **Power Apps** under available triggers.
2. Select **"Power Apps (V2)"** as your trigger.
3. This trigger allows the flow to start when an event occurs in your app.

Step 3: Add an Action to the Flow

1. Click **"New Step"** to define what should happen next.
2. Choose an action based on what you want your flow to do. Common actions include:

- **Send an email notification** when a user submits a form.
- **Create a record** in SharePoint or a database.
- **Update an Excel file** with new data.

1. Configure the action by filling in required details (e.g., recipient email, message content, or database fields).

Step 4: Pass Data from Power Apps to Power Automate

1. In your chosen action, click **"Ask in Power Apps"** to create a dynamic input field.
2. This allows your Power App to send specific data (such as a name, email, or request ID) to Power Automate.
3. Save your flow once all steps are correctly configured.

Step 5: Connect the Flow to Power Apps

1. Open **Power Apps** and select the app you want to automate.
2. Go to the screen where you need automation (such as a submit button).
3. Select the button or element and navigate to the **On Select** property.
4. Type the following formula:

```
'FlowName'.Run(Parameter1, Parameter2)
```

- Replace Flow Name with the actual name of your Power Automate flow.
- Replace Parameter1, Parameter2 with the actual data you want to pass from Power Apps.

Step 6: Test and Deploy the Flow

1. Run your Power App and perform the action that triggers the flow.
2. Check Power Automate to ensure the flow runs successfully.
3. If everything works as expected, save and publish your app.

Example: Automating Email Notifications from Power Apps

Let's say you have an app where users submit feedback. Instead of manually checking responses, you want to **automatically receive an email** whenever new feedback is submitted.

Steps to Build This Automation:

1. **In Power Automate:**

- Create a new instant flow.
- Select **PowerApps (V2)** as the trigger.
- Add a **Send an email (Outlook 365)** action.
- Set the recipient email to **"Ask in PowerApps"** to allow dynamic input.
- Add the subject and body fields, also set to receive values from Power Apps.
- Save the flow.

1. **In Power Apps:**

- Insert a **Button** on the feedback submission screen.
- Select the button and modify the **On Select** property with:

```
'SendEmailFlow'.Run(User().Email, TextInput1.Text)
```

- This ensures that when the button is pressed, Power Automate receives the user's email and feedback.

1. **Test the app:**

- Enter feedback in the text box and press submit.
- Check your email to confirm that the notification was sent.

This simple integration eliminates **manual email tracking** and ensures every response is instantly delivered.

Best Practices for Power Apps and Power Automate Integration

1. Keep Workflows Simple and Clear

Avoid overly complex flows. Stick to **a clear sequence of actions** to ensure the automation remains easy to manage and troubleshoot.

2. Use Meaningful Names

When naming flows, variables, and parameters, use **descriptive names** to make it easier to understand what each element does.

3. Monitor and Optimize Performance

Regularly check flow history in Power Automate to ensure everything runs **without delays or errors**. Optimize slow workflows by **removing unnecessary steps**.

4. Test Thoroughly Before Deployment

Before rolling out an automation, **test it multiple times** to verify that it behaves as expected under different conditions.

5. Ensure Data Security

Since Power Automate handles sensitive information, always configure **proper security settings** to restrict unauthorized access.

7.3 Creating Flow-Based Automations from Power Apps

Automation has become a vital part of modern applications, helping to reduce manual effort, improve accuracy, and speed up processes. By integrating **flow-based automations** into Power Apps, you can create dynamic applications that not only collect data but also trigger real-time actions, ensuring seamless workflows without human intervention.

Power Apps and **Power Automate** work hand in hand to provide these automated solutions. Whether you need to send emails, update databases, notify users, or process approvals, flow-based automation makes it possible with just a few clicks.

Why Use Flow-Based Automations in Power Apps?

Instead of relying on users to manually complete every task, **flowbased automation** allows Power Apps to initiate actions automatically. This reduces time-consuming tasks, eliminates repetitive work, and ensures consistency. Some key benefits include:

- **Real-time updates** without the need for manual intervention.
- **Reduced human errors** by automating calculations, approvals, and notifications.
- **Enhanced user experience** by making applications more responsive and intelligent.
- **Seamless integration** with various services such as SharePoint, Outlook, SQL databases, and more.

For example, when a customer submits a request through a Power App, a flow can be triggered to send a confirmation email, update a database, and notify the relevant department—all without any manual effort.

Understanding Flow-Based Automations

A **flow** is an automated sequence of actions that gets triggered based on an event. When you create a flow from Power Apps, it follows a clear structure:

1. **Trigger:** An event occurs in Power Apps (e.g., a button is pressed).
2. **Action:** The flow executes predefined tasks (e.g., send an email, update a record).
3. **Output:** The results are sent back to Power Apps or stored in another system.

By following these steps, you can create flows that perform multiple actions within seconds, making your apps smarter and more efficient.

Step-by-Step Guide to Creating Flow-Based Automations

Let's walk through the process of building an automated flow from Power Apps.

Step 1: Open Power Automate and Start a New Flow

1. Sign in to **Power Automate** using your Microsoft account.
2. Click **"Create"** and choose **"Instant cloud flow"** to build an automation that runs on demand.
3. In the next screen, select **"PowerApps (V2)"** as the flow trigger.
4. Give your flow a meaningful name, such as **"Process Request Flow"**, and click **"Create"**.

Step 2: Define the Trigger from Power Apps

1. Once the flow designer opens, click on **"PowerApps (V2)"** to configure it as the starting point.
2. This trigger will allow Power Apps to send data to Power Automate whenever an action occurs in the app.

Step 3: Add Actions to the Flow

Now, define what the flow should do after being triggered from Power Apps. Some common actions include:

- **Sending an email** to notify users.
- **Updating a SharePoint list** with new data.

- **Creating a record** in a database.
- **Sending a Teams notification** when a request is submitted.

To add an action:

1. Click **"New Step"** and choose an action, such as **"Send an email"** (Outlook 365).
2. Configure the details (recipient, subject, and message body).
3. If needed, click **"Ask in PowerApps"** to allow the app to pass values dynamically.

Step 4: Pass Data from Power Apps to Power Automate

To make your flow dynamic, allow Power Apps to send specific data to Power Automate.

1. In the action settings, click on a required field (e.g., email address).
2. Select **"Ask in PowerApps"** to create an input field that will receive data from Power Apps.
3. Repeat this for any other fields that need dynamic input.

For example, if a user submits a request, Power Apps can send their name, email, and request details to Power Automate, which then processes the data accordingly.

Step 5: Save and Test Your Flow

1. Click **"Save"** to store your automation.
2. Click **"Test"** and select **"Manually trigger"** to check if it runs correctly.
3. If everything works as expected, your flow is ready to be linked

to Power Apps.

Step 6: Connect the Flow to Power Apps

1. Open **Power Apps** and navigate to the screen where you need automation.
2. Select the button or control that should trigger the flow (e.g., a **Submit** button).
3. In the **On Select** property of the button, type:

```
'ProcessRequestFlow'.Run(TextInput1.Text, TextInput2.Text)
```

- Replace Process Request Flow with the actual name of your flow.
- Replace TextInput1.Text, TextInput2.Text with the fields from Power Apps that will pass data to the flow.

1. Save and test your app to ensure the flow is executed correctly when the button is clicked.

Example: Automating Approval Requests in Power Apps

Let's consider a scenario where employees submit leave requests using Power Apps. Instead of manually reviewing requests, a **flow-based automation** can be created to:

- **Send the request to a manager** for approval.
- **Notify the employee** about the status.
- **Update the records** in a SharePoint list.

Steps to Build This Flow:

1. **Create a flow** in Power Automate and select **PowerApps (V2)** as the trigger.
2. **Add an approval action** to request the manager's response.
3. **Set up a conditional step:**

- If approved, send an email to the employee and update the database.
- If rejected, notify the employee with a reason.

1. **Pass values from Power Apps** for dynamic responses.
2. **Save and connect** the flow to Power Apps.

This setup ensures a **smooth and transparent approval process** without requiring manual follow-ups.

Best Practices for Creating Flow-Based Automations

1. Keep Flows Simple and Clear

Ensure each flow has a **clear purpose** and avoid unnecessary steps to improve performance.

2. Use Meaningful Names for Flows and Actions

Label flows and actions descriptively to make troubleshooting and maintenance easier.

3. Monitor and Optimize Performance

Check the flow history in Power Automate to identify **bottlenecks or errors**, and refine the process accordingly.

4. Test Before Deployment

Run multiple tests to confirm the automation **behaves correctly** in all scenarios before launching it.

5. Secure Data Access

Use role-based permissions to prevent unauthorized users from triggering sensitive flows.

7.4 Example: Automating Data Entry and Notifications

Handling data manually can be time-consuming, prone to mistakes, and frustrating. Whether it's updating a database, logging requests, or sending notifications, relying on manual work often leads to errors and delays. This is where **automation** steps in—by reducing the need for human intervention, it ensures accuracy, speeds up processes, and keeps everything running smoothly.

By using **Power Automate** with **Power Apps**, you can build a system that **automatically records data** and sends **real-time notifications** when needed. In this section, we will create an automation that collects user-submitted data in Power Apps, logs it into a SharePoint list (or another database), and sends a notification to a designated recipient.

Why Automate Data Entry and Notifications?

Automation is more than just convenience—it's a **powerful tool** that helps eliminate inefficiencies and ensures **real-time communication**. Here are some reasons why automating these tasks can be a game changer:

- **Saves time:** No more entering information manually or sending notifications by hand.
- **Reduces errors:** Automation ensures data is captured correctly every time.
- **Enhances productivity:** Users can focus on important work instead of repetitive tasks.
- **Improves communication:** Instant alerts keep everyone informed without delays.

For example, if a user submits a **service request** through Power Apps, automation can immediately:

1. Log the request into a database.
2. Send an email to the support team.
3. Notify the user about the request status.

Let's walk through how to create this system step by step.

Step-by-Step Guide to Automating Data Entry and Notifications

Step 1: Create a Power Apps Form

To begin, design a simple form in Power Apps where users can submit data.

1. Open **Power Apps** and create a **new canvas app**.
2. Add a **Text Input** field for data entry (e.g., name, email, request details).
3. Insert a **Button** that users can click to submit their information.
4. Name the button **"Submit Request"** for clarity.

Step 2: Create a Flow in Power Automate

Now, we will set up an automation that takes the submitted data and processes it.

1. Open **Power Automate** and click **"Create"**.
2. Choose **"Instant cloud flow"** and select **PowerApps (V2)** as the trigger.
3. Name the flow **"Log Request and Notify"**, then click **"Create"**.

Step 3: Capture Data from Power Apps

To ensure Power Automate receives the data from Power Apps:

1. Click on the **PowerApps (V2) trigger** in the flow.
2. For each required field (e.g., Name, Email, Request Details), select **"Ask in PowerApps"**.
3. This step allows Power Apps to send values directly to Power Automate when the button is clicked.

Step 4: Store Data in a SharePoint List (or Another Database)

Now, we will save the submitted information into a database.

1. Click **"New Step"** and select **"Create Item"** (if using SharePoint).
2. Choose your **SharePoint site** and select the **list** where the data should be saved.
3. Map the fields:

- **Title:** User's name (or another relevant identifier).
- **Email:** The submitted email address.
- **Request Details:** The message or request description.

1. If using a different database (SQL, Dataverse, Excel), select the corresponding action and map the fields similarly.

Step 5: Send a Notification to the User and Team

Once the data is stored, the flow should notify both the user and the relevant team.

1. Click **"New Step"** and choose **"Send an Email (Outlook 365)"**.
2. Set the recipient to the email provided by the user (using dynamic content).
3. Craft a **confirmation message**:

- Subject: **"Your Request Has Been Received"**
- Body:

```
Hello [User's Name],
We have received your request. Our team will review it and
get back to you shortly.
Request Details: [Request Description]
Thank you for reaching out!
```

1. Click **"New Step"** and add another email action to notify the support team.
2. Set the **recipient** to the team's shared inbox and include details of the request.

Step 6: Connect the Flow to Power Apps

Now, return to **Power Apps** and link the flow to the **Submit Request** button.

1. Select the button and open the **On Select** property.
2. Use the following formula to trigger the flow:

```
'LogRequestAndNotify'.Run(NameInput.Text, EmailInput.Text,
RequestInput.Text)
```

1. Replace the field names accordingly based on your Power Apps setup.
2. Save and test the application by submitting a request.

Testing and Validation

After setting up the automation, **testing** is essential to ensure everything functions correctly.

1. Open Power Apps and **submit a test request**.
2. Check if the data is **saved** correctly in the database.
3. Confirm that the **user receives a confirmation email**.
4. Ensure the **team gets a notification** about the new request.
5. Review the Power Automate flow history to spot any errors or improvements.

If something doesn't work as expected, check:

- Whether Power Apps is correctly sending data to Power Automate.
- If the flow is **mapping the fields correctly** to the database.
- Whether email notifications are **sent to the right recipients**.

Example Use Cases for Automated Data Entry and Notifications

1. Employee Leave Requests

Employees can submit leave requests through Power Apps. Automation then:

- Logs the request into a **SharePoint list**.
- Sends an **approval request** to the manager.
- Notifies the employee once approved or rejected.

2. Customer Support Ticketing

Customers submit issues through Power Apps, and the flow:

- Stores the complaint in a **database**.
- Sends a **confirmation email** to the customer.
- Notifies the **support team** for quick action.

3. Event Registration

Users register for an event, and automation:

- Saves their information in a **registration list**.
- Sends a **confirmation email** with event details.
- Alerts the **organizing team** about new registrations.

7.5 Tips for Integration

Integrating Power Automate with other tools, such as **Power Apps, SharePoint, Microsoft Teams, or Outlook**, can significantly enhance efficiency and streamline workflows. However, successful integration requires careful planning, attention to detail, and a clear understanding of how different components interact.

To ensure smooth and effective automation, it's essential to follow best practices and apply key strategies. Below, we will explore practical tips to help you integrate Power Automate seamlessly into your system, making processes more reliable and effortless.

1. Define a Clear Purpose for Your Automation

Before setting up an integration, take the time to **identify the goal** of your automation. Ask yourself:

- What specific task do you want to automate?
- How will automation improve efficiency?
- Which applications or services need to be connected?

For example, if you want to **automate approval workflows**, determine whether the data comes from **Power Apps**, is stored in **SharePoint**, and requires approval via **Outlook or Teams notifications**. Clearly outlining your objectives will help you design a flow that meets business needs without unnecessary complexity.

2. Choose the Right Triggers and Actions

Power Automate operates based on **triggers** (events that start a flow) and **actions** (tasks executed after the trigger). Selecting the correct ones ensures a seamless connection between different services.

- **Instant triggers**: Used for on-demand actions, such as submitting a form in Power Apps.
- **Scheduled triggers**: Best for tasks that need to run at specific times, like daily reports.
- **Automated triggers**: Ideal for real-time actions, such as receiving an email or updating a database.

For example, if you need to **sync customer records** between Power Apps and a database, use the **"When an item is created or modified"** trigger in SharePoint or Dataverse to ensure automatic updates without manual intervention.

3. Keep Flows Simple and Organized

A well-structured flow is **easier to manage, troubleshoot, and optimize**. Overcomplicated automations can cause unexpected failures, making it difficult to identify issues. Follow these best practices:

- **Break down large workflows** into smaller, manageable flows when possible.
- **Use meaningful names** for actions and variables to make the flow easier to understand.
- **Test each step** before finalizing the entire workflow to catch potential errors early.
- **Document your flow** so team members can understand and maintain it.

For example, instead of creating a **single flow with multiple conditional branches**, consider separating approval, data entry, and notifications into different flows. This improves performance and makes troubleshooting simpler.

4. Ensure Data Security and Access Control

When integrating multiple applications, it's essential to protect sensitive information and **limit access to authorized users**.

- **Use role-based permissions** to ensure only approved users can trigger or modify flows.
- **Encrypt sensitive data** when transferring information between

systems.

- **Monitor access logs** to track automation usage and detect potential security risks.

For example, when integrating **Power Automate with SharePoint**, restrict access so that only managers can approve requests, while employees can only submit forms. This ensures that confidential information is handled appropriately.

5. Optimize for Performance and Efficiency

To keep automations running smoothly, consider performance optimization techniques:

- **Limit unnecessary actions** to reduce processing time.
- **Use parallel branching** when possible to perform multiple tasks at the same time.
- **Avoid excessive API calls** to prevent system overload.
- **Monitor flow execution history** to detect slow-running processes.

For instance, if a workflow **updates hundreds of records**, use **batch processing** instead of updating each record individually. This significantly improves execution speed and reduces system strain.

6. Plan for Error Handling and Troubleshooting

Even the best-designed workflows can encounter errors due to network issues, incorrect data inputs, or system limitations. Implementing **error handling mechanisms** ensures that automations continue running smoothly.

- Use **"Configure Run After" settings** to specify actions when a step fails.
- **Set up notifications for failures** so issues can be addressed quickly.
- **Log errors in a centralized location** (e.g., SharePoint list or database) for easy tracking.
- **Test and refine automations regularly** to identify potential points of failure.

For example, if an automated **email notification fails**, instead of stopping the entire workflow, set up an alternate action that logs the failure and sends an alert to the IT team.

7. Test and Validate Integrations Before Deployment

Before rolling out automation to all users, thorough **testing** is crucial to ensure everything functions correctly.

- **Run multiple test cases** using different data inputs.
- **Simulate real-world scenarios** to check if automations respond correctly.
- **Ensure all integrated applications communicate smoothly**.
- **Get feedback from users** to identify potential improvements.

For example, if you're integrating **Power Automate with Teams notifications**, verify that messages reach the intended recipients without delays. Testing helps prevent disruptions and ensures a seamless experience for users.

8. Regularly Review and Improve Workflows

Automation should be treated as a continuous improvement process. As business needs change, **workflows should be updated** to remain relevant and efficient.

- **Review automation performance** periodically to detect inefficiencies.
- **Analyze user feedback** to identify areas for improvement.
- **Update integrations** when new features or improvements are available.
- **Retire outdated workflows** that are no longer useful.

For instance, if a workflow for **customer inquiries** is causing delays, consider modifying it to include **AI-based responses** or integrating a chatbot for faster replies.

Chapter 8: Power Apps and Power BI Integration

8.1 Overview of Power BI

Data has the power to transform the way decisions are made. Whether in business, education, healthcare, or any other industry, understanding data helps in **making informed choices, predicting trends, and improving efficiency**. However, raw data by itself can be overwhelming, especially when dealing with large volumes of information. This is where **Power BI** comes in.

Power BI is a **data visualization and business intelligence tool** developed by Microsoft. It allows users to **collect, analyze, and present data** in a clear and interactive way. With its easy-to-use interface, Power BI turns complex datasets into meaningful insights through **charts, graphs, dashboards, and reports**.

When integrated with Power Apps, **users can interact with data dynamically**, allowing for a seamless flow of information between applications and reports. Instead of relying on separate tools for data entry and visualization, this integration creates a **unified experience** where users can **update, analyze, and act on data—all from a single platform**.

1. Why Use Power BI?

1.1 Transforming Raw Data into Insights

Power BI helps turn **plain numbers into meaningful visual stories**. Instead of scrolling through endless rows of data, users can see **clear trends, patterns, and comparisons** in charts and dashboards.

1.2 Connecting Data from Multiple Sources

Data often comes from different places—Excel files, databases, cloud services, and even real-time streaming sources. Power BI **combines all this information** into one platform, making analysis easier and more efficient.

1.3 Real-Time Monitoring

With **live dashboards**, Power BI provides up-to-date insights. Whether tracking sales performance, customer feedback, or operational efficiency, businesses can **make quick decisions based on real-time data**.

1.4 User-Friendly and Interactive

One of the biggest strengths of Power BI is its **intuitive design**. Users with little technical knowledge can still create powerful reports, while advanced users can dig deeper into **custom visualizations and complex data models**.

1.5 Secure and Scalable

Data security is a major concern in any organization. Power BI ensures **strong security measures** through role-based access, encryption, and cloud protection. It also **scales easily**, making it suitable for both small teams and large enterprises.

2. Key Components of Power BI

2.1 Power BI Desktop

This is the **main application** where users create reports and visualizations. It allows for **data modeling, transformations, and interactive reports**, which can later be published to the cloud or shared with others.

2.2 Power BI Service (Cloud-Based Platform)

The Power BI Service is a **web-based platform** where reports and dashboards are stored, shared, and accessed online. It allows teams to **collaborate on reports**, set up scheduled refreshes, and view live data from anywhere.

2.3 Power BI Mobile App

For those who need access to reports on the go, Power BI's mobile app allows users to **view dashboards and reports on their smartphones and tablets**, ensuring data is always available when needed.

2.4 Power BI Gateway

This feature is essential for businesses that need to **connect cloud based Power BI reports with on-premises data sources**. It enables **secure data transfers** without exposing sensitive information.

2.5 Power BI Embedded

For developers who want to integrate Power BI reports directly into **custom applications**, this feature provides API access to embed reports within other software platforms.

3. How Power BI Works

Step 1: Importing Data

Power BI allows users to **import data from multiple sources**, including:

- Excel spreadsheets
- SQL databases
- Cloud platforms like Azure and Google Analytics
- APIs and web-based sources

Step 2: Transforming Data

Raw data is often messy or incomplete. Power BI provides tools to **clean, filter, and shape** the data before using it in reports. Users can **remove errors, combine data tables, and create calculated columns** for better analysis.

Step 3: Creating Visualizations

Once the data is ready, Power BI offers a variety of visual tools, including:

- Bar charts, pie charts, and line graphs
- Maps for geographic data
- Tables and matrices for structured information
- Custom visuals for unique reporting needs

Users can **drag and drop elements** to build reports without needing complex programming.

Step 4: Building Dashboards

Dashboards allow users to **combine multiple visualizations** into a single view. This makes it easy to track **performance metrics, trends, and KPIs** at a glance.

Step 5: Sharing and Collaborating

Reports can be **published to the Power BI Service**, where teams can **collaborate, share insights, and set up automated data refreshes** to keep information up to date.

4. Power BI and Power Apps Integration

While Power BI focuses on **data analysis and visualization**, Power Apps is designed to **build custom applications for data collection and business processes**. Integrating the two allows users to **not only view insights but also take action directly from reports**.
For example:

- A sales manager viewing a Power BI report on customer orders can use **a connected Power App** to **update order details directly** without switching applications.
- A service technician can see **real-time equipment performance data** and submit **repair requests** from the same dashboard.

This integration **bridges the gap** between reporting and action, making businesses more responsive and efficient.

8.2 Embedding Power BI Reports in Power Apps

Data plays a crucial role in decision-making, and businesses thrive when they can access and act on insights quickly. **Embedding Power BI reports into Power Apps** allows users to **interact with live data, analyze trends, and make informed choices**—all within a single application. Instead of switching between platforms, users can view detailed reports and take immediate action without interruptions.

By integrating Power BI with Power Apps, businesses create a **seamless experience where data drives actions**. Whether it's tracking sales, monitoring employee performance, or analyzing customer feedback, embedding reports into apps ensures **users get**

the right insights at the right time.

1. Why Embed Power BI in Power Apps?

1.1 Streamlined Workflow

Having reports embedded directly in an app means users **don't need to leave the application** to access insights. This speeds up decision-making and ensures efficiency.

1.2 Real-Time Data at Your Fingertips

Instead of relying on outdated reports, users can interact with **live data visualizations**, ensuring they make decisions based on the most up-to-date information.

1.3 Action-Oriented Insights

Rather than just analyzing numbers, users can **act on insights immediately**. For example, a manager reviewing a sales report can update an order or approve a discount directly within the same app.

1.4 User-Friendly and Interactive

Embedded Power BI reports allow users to **filter, drill down, and explore data interactively**, giving them **a customized experience based on their needs**.

1.5 Secure and Controlled Access

By embedding reports within Power Apps, administrators can **control access based on roles**, ensuring that only authorized users can view specific data.

2. How to Embed Power BI Reports in Power Apps

Step 1: Prepare the Power BI Report

Before embedding, ensure the Power BI report is **published and accessible**.

1. Open **Power BI Desktop** and create the required report.
2. Apply filters, formatting, and any interactive elements needed.
3. Click on **Publish** and select a destination workspace in Power BI Service.

Step 2: Get the Power BI Report URL or Embed Code

1. Go to **Power BI Service** and locate the published report.
2. Click on the **Share** button or navigate to the **File > Embed Report** option.
3. Copy the **report URL or embed link** needed for integration.

Step 3: Open Power Apps and Add a Power BI Control

1. In **Power Apps**, open an existing app or create a new one.
2. Navigate to the screen where the report will be embedded.
3. Click on **Insert** in the top menu and select **Power BI tile** from the available controls.

Step 4: Connect the Power BI Report to Power Apps

1. Select the **Power BI tile** added to the app.
2. Under **Properties**, locate the section where you can **paste the report URL or embed link**.
3. Choose the **workspace** where the report is stored.
4. Select the **specific report and tile** to display.

Step 5: Customize the Embedded Report

1. Adjust the size and position of the report within Power Apps.
2. Modify visibility settings to ensure it only appears when needed.
3. Set filters to **display relevant data to different users based on their roles**.

Step 6: Test and Publish the App

1. Run the app in preview mode to verify that the report loads correctly.
2. Interact with the report by **applying filters and checking real time updates**.
3. Make any necessary adjustments before publishing the app for use.

3. Best Practices for Embedding Power BI in Power Apps

1. Optimize Report Performance

Keep reports **lightweight and efficient** by limiting excessive data and visuals. Use **data aggregation** to avoid slow loading times.

2. Ensure Data Security

Configure **role-based access control** so that only authorized users can view specific reports. Use **Power BI security settings** to restrict sensitive data.

3. Use Responsive Design

Make sure embedded reports are **optimized for different screen sizes**, including desktops, tablets, and mobile devices.

4. Keep Reports Relevant to the App's Purpose

Only embed **essential** reports that align with the app's functionality. Avoid cluttering the interface with unnecessary visualizations.

5. Regularly Update Reports

Ensure the embedded report **refreshes automatically** so users always see the latest data without needing manual updates.

8.3 Creating Interactive Dashboards with Power BI

Data has the power to tell a story, but only if it is presented in a way that is easy to understand. **An interactive dashboard in Power BI does more than just display numbers—it transforms raw data into meaningful insights.** It allows users to engage with information dynamically, filter results in real-time, and make decisions with confidence.

A well-designed dashboard can bring clarity to complex data, enabling businesses to **track performance, identify trends, and respond quickly to changes.** Whether you are monitoring sales, customer feedback, or operational efficiency, an interactive dashboard ensures that insights are always within reach.

1. What Makes a Dashboard Interactive?

An interactive dashboard does not just display static charts. It **responds to user input, refreshes data in real-time, and provides multiple ways to explore information.** Here's what makes a dashboard interactive:

1.1 Dynamic Filters and Slicers

Users can filter data instantly based on specific criteria, such as date range, category, or region. This allows for **personalized insights tailored to individual needs.**

1.2 Drill-Through and Drill-Down Features

Instead of looking at a broad summary, users can **click on data points to reveal deeper insights.** For example, clicking on a sales figure can break it down by product or location.

1.3 Real-Time Data Updates

Dashboards connected to live data sources can **update automatically, ensuring users always see the latest information.**

1.4 Interactive Visuals

Charts, graphs, and maps are not just static images. **They respond to user interactions, making it easy to explore trends and patterns.**

2. How to Create an Interactive Dashboard in Power BI

Step 1: Define the Purpose of the Dashboard

Before designing, clarify **what the dashboard will be used for and who will use it.**

- Is it for sales tracking, customer insights, or financial reporting?
- What key performance indicators (KPIs) should be included?
- Who needs access to the data, and what level of detail do they require?

Step 2: Collect and Connect Data Sources

1. Open **Power BI Desktop** and click on **Get Data**.
2. Choose the relevant data source (Excel, SQL Server, SharePoint, etc.).
3. Load the data and use **Power Query** to clean, transform, and structure it for analysis.
4. Ensure that all data is properly formatted and relationships between tables are correctly defined.

Step 3: Design the Dashboard Layout

1. Select a **blank report canvas** and plan the placement of visuals.
2. Use **consistent colors, fonts, and spacing** to create a clean and professional look.
3. Arrange visuals in a way that tells a clear story—**start with summary metrics and allow deeper exploration through drill-downs.**

Step 4: Add Interactive Visuals

1. Click on **Visualizations** and choose the right type of chart for each data point:

- **Bar charts** for comparisons
- **Line graphs** for trends over time
- **Maps** for geographic data
- **Tables and matrix views** for detailed information

1. Drag fields into the visualization fields to populate them with data.
2. Adjust colors, labels, and tooltips for clarity.

Step 5: Implement Filters and Slicers

1. Add slicers for filtering data by **date, category, region, or any other criteria.**
2. Use **cross-filtering** so selecting one visual updates the rest of the dashboard.
3. Configure drill-through options to **allow users to explore more details with a click.**

Step 6: Set Up Real-Time Data Updates

1. If using live data, enable **automatic refresh settings** in Power BI Service.
2. Schedule regular updates to keep the dashboard current.

Step /: Test and Optimize the Dashboard

1. Preview the dashboard from the user's perspective.
2. Check if **filters and interactions work smoothly.**
3. Optimize performance by **reducing the number of visuals or optimizing data queries.**

Step 8: Publish and Share the Dashboard

1. Save the file and click on **Publish** to upload it to Power BI Service.
2. Share the dashboard with relevant users by adjusting access permissions.
3. Embed the dashboard in **Power Apps** or **Microsoft Teams** for easy access.

8.4 Using Power BI Data for Decision-Making in Power Apps

Every decision in a business shapes its future, and the right data can make all the difference. Without accurate insights, decisions are based on guesswork, leading to wasted resources and missed opportunities. This is where **Power BI and Power Apps come together**—offering a seamless way to transform raw data into smart, informed actions.

Power BI provides **deep insights through real-time reports and dashboards**, while Power Apps allows users to interact with that data in a **practical, action-driven environment.** By integrating Power BI data into Power Apps, businesses can create **intelligent applications** that not only display insights but also enable users to act on them immediately.

1. Why Use Power BI Data in Power Apps?

1.1 Turning Insights into Actions

A report on sales trends is valuable, but the ability to **place a new order directly from the report makes it even more powerful.** This integration allows businesses to **act on insights instantly.**

1.2 Reducing Errors and Improving Efficiency

By linking Power BI data with Power Apps, employees no longer have to manually transfer data between systems. **Automated data flow eliminates mistakes and saves time.**

1.3 Enhancing Decision-Making with Real-Time Data

Instead of relying on outdated spreadsheets or static reports, Power Apps users can access **up-to-the-minute data** from Power BI and make decisions based on the latest trends.

2. How to Use Power BI Data in Power Apps

Step 1: Prepare Power BI Data for Integration

Before connecting Power BI to Power Apps, ensure the data is **structured and relevant** for decision-making.

1. Open **Power BI Desktop** and load your dataset.
2. Clean the data using **Power Query** to remove unnecessary fields and errors.
3. Create meaningful reports with the most **relevant charts, tables, and KPIs.**
4. Publish the report to **Power BI Service**, making sure it is accessible to the right users.

Step 2: Connect Power BI Data to Power Apps

1. Open **Power Apps Studio** and create a new app or open an existing one.
2. Click on **Data** from the left panel and select **Add Data**.
3. Search for **Power BI** and connect it to your app.
4. Choose the dataset or report that contains the data you want to use.
5. Add **Power BI tiles** or **data tables** to display insights within the app.

199

Step 3: Build Interactive Features Based on Data

1. Add **filters** and **search functions** so users can explore the data easily.
2. Use **conditional formatting** to highlight important insights (e.g., if sales drop below a threshold, it turns red).
3. Enable **real-time updates** so that users always see the most recent data.
4. Link data to actions—such as allowing users to **place orders, schedule meetings, or submit reports** based on Power BI insights.

Step 4: Automate Actions with Power Automate

To make the app even more powerful, integrate **Power Automate** to trigger workflows based on Power BI data.

1. Open **Power Automate** and create a new flow.
2. Choose a **Power BI trigger**, such as "When data is updated in a dataset."
3. Define an action, like **sending an email alert or updating a record in Power Apps**.
4. Test the automation to ensure it runs smoothly.

Step 5: Test and Deploy the App

1. **Check the app's performance** to ensure it loads quickly and displays data accurately.
2. Test different **user roles and permissions** to ensure security.
3. Get feedback from users and make improvements.
4. Publish the app and provide training to users on how to use the

integrated Power BI insights.

8.5 Sharing Data and Visualizations Seamlessly

Data becomes truly powerful when it is shared effectively. The insights hidden in reports and visualizations can drive better decisions, but if they remain locked away in individual systems, their potential is wasted. **Seamless data sharing ensures that the right people have access to the right information at the right time.**

Integrating Power BI with Power Apps allows businesses to **break down barriers between data and action.** Instead of static reports sitting in dashboards, insights can be embedded directly into applications where employees can use them immediately. Whether it's sales teams needing customer insights or managers tracking performance, making data accessible transforms the way businesses operate.

This chapter explores the best ways to **share data and visualizations effortlessly**, ensuring that your team stays informed, engaged, and empowered.

1. Why Seamless Data Sharing Matters

1.1 Eliminating Data Silos

When different teams rely on separate systems, valuable information can be **trapped in isolated databases, leading to miscommunication and inefficiencies.** Seamless data sharing ensures that insights flow across departments effortlessly.

1.2 Speeding Up Decision-Making

Real-time access to reports and visualizations enables employees to **act quickly** without waiting for manual updates or approvals.

1.3 Improving Collaboration

Sharing interactive reports fosters teamwork by **giving everyone access to the same data**—ensuring decisions are based on facts, not assumptions.

1.4 Enhancing Transparency

When data is easily accessible, organizations can **build trust** among employees, stakeholders, and customers by providing clear insights into performance and progress.

2. How to Share Power BI Reports and Visualizations

Step 1: Publish Reports to Power BI Service

Before sharing reports, ensure they are accessible through Power BI Service.

1. Open **Power BI Desktop** and finalize your report.
2. Click on **Publish** and select the appropriate **workspace** in Power BI Service.
3. Ensure the report is updated with **real-time data connections** to keep insights current.

Step 2: Set Up Permissions for Secure Access

1. Open Power BI Service and go to the **report or dashboard** you want to share.
2. Click on **Share** and enter the **email addresses** of the users who need access.
3. Select **view-only** or **edit** permissions based on the level of access required.
4. Enable **row-level security (RLS)** if different users should see only specific parts of the data.

Step 3: Embed Power BI Reports in Power Apps

For a seamless experience, embed Power BI reports directly into Power Apps so users can interact with data within their workflow.

1. Open **Power Apps Studio** and select your app.
2. Click on **Insert > Charts > Power BI Tile** to add a Power BI report.
3. Connect to your Power BI workspace and choose the desired report.
4. Adjust the size and positioning for better usability.
5. Test the integration to ensure data updates in real-time.

Step 4: Automate Data Sharing with Power Automate

Automating report distribution ensures that users receive insights without manual intervention.

1. Open **Power Automate** and create a new flow.
2. Select **Power BI as the trigger** (e.g., "When a report is re-

freshed").

3. Choose an action, such as **sending an email, updating a database, or generating a notification** in Power Apps.
4. Configure the details and test the workflow to confirm automation runs smoothly.

Step 5: Export and Share Reports in Different Formats

For users who prefer offline access, Power BI reports can be shared in multiple formats.

1. Open the report in Power BI Service.
2. Click on **Export** and choose a format:

- **PDF** for printable reports
- **Excel** for further data analysis
- **PowerPoint** for presentations

1. Send the exported report via email or upload it to a shared drive.

Tips for Sharing Data Effectively

1. Keep Data Up-to-Date

Ensure that reports refresh automatically so users always see the most recent insights. Use **scheduled refresh settings** in Power BI to automate updates.

2. Maintain Security and Compliance

Not all users should have access to sensitive data. Use **role-based permissions and encryption** to protect confidential information.

3. Ensure Reports Are User-Friendly

Complicated dashboards can overwhelm users. Focus on **clarity, simplicity, and ease of navigation** so insights are easy to understand.

4. Use Interactive Elements

Enable users to filter, search, and drill down into reports **without needing technical expertise**. This enhances engagement and usability.

5. Track Engagement and Feedback

Monitor how reports are being used and gather feedback from users. **Regular improvements** ensure that data sharing remains effective.

Chapter 9: Security and Permissions

9.1 Introduction to Security in Power Apps

Security is the backbone of any digital application. Without proper security measures, sensitive data can be exposed, unauthorized users can gain access, and an organization's operations can be put at risk. **Power Apps, as a powerful low-code platform, allows businesses to build applications that integrate with various data sources— but without the right security configurations, those applications can become vulnerable.**

Security in Power Apps is not just about protecting data but also about ensuring that only the right people can access the right information at the right time. Whether you're dealing with financial records, customer data, or confidential business strategies, implementing **strong security controls** is essential to prevent unauthorized access, data breaches, and compliance violations.

1. Why Security Matters in Power Apps

1.1 Protecting Sensitive Information

Organizations store valuable data in Power Apps, from customer details to financial records. Without proper security measures, this data could end up in the wrong hands. Ensuring that only **authorized users** can access critical data is a fundamental step in securing your applications.

1.2 Preventing Unauthorized Access

Applications often involve multiple users, from employees to external partners. By setting up **role-based access control**, organizations can define who can view, edit, or delete information, preventing unauthorized actions.

1.3 Ensuring Compliance

Many businesses must comply with **data protection laws** such as GDPR, HIPAA, or internal company policies. Implementing security features in Power Apps helps organizations stay compliant and avoid legal consequences.

1.4 Reducing Risk of Data Breaches

Cybersecurity threats are increasing, and businesses must be proactive. By securing Power Apps, organizations can **minimize risks** and ensure their data remains protected from cyber-attacks and accidental leaks.

2. Understanding Security in Power Apps

Power Apps provides multiple layers of security to protect applications and data. Here's an overview of the key security components:

2.1 Role-Based Access Control (RBAC)

RBAC allows administrators to **assign specific roles to users** based on their responsibilities. Instead of giving all users full access, permissions are granted based on what each person needs.

- **Owner** – Has full control over the app, including editing, deleting, and sharing permissions.
- **Contributor** – Can edit the app but cannot manage permissions.
- **User** – Can access and use the app but cannot modify it.
- **Guest** – Limited access, typically for external users.

2.2 Data Security with Dataverse

Power Apps integrates with **Microsoft Dataverse**, a secure data storage solution. Dataverse includes **row-level security**, meaning data access can be restricted at the record level. This ensures that employees only see the data they are authorized to view.

- **Table Permissions** – Control access at the database level.
- **Row-Level Security (RLS)** – Restrict access to specific records based on user roles.
- **Field-Level Security** – Protect specific fields within a record from unauthorized viewing.

2.3 *Authentication and Identity Management*

Authentication ensures that only verified users can access Power Apps. Power Apps supports **Microsoft Entra ID (formerly Azure Active Directory)** for authentication, allowing businesses to enforce **multifactor authentication (MFA)** and **single sign-on (SSO)** for added security.

- **MFA** – Requires an additional layer of authentication, such as a mobile code or fingerprint, to verify user identity.
- **SSO** – Allows users to log in once and gain access to multiple applications without re-entering credentials.

2.4 *Secure Sharing and Permissions*

When sharing a Power App, it's crucial to **control access permissions** properly. Power Apps allows you to:

- Share apps only with **specific users or groups** instead of making them public.
- Restrict **editing rights** to only a few trusted individuals.
- Use **conditional access policies** to prevent unauthorized logins from unknown devices.

3. Step-by-Step Guide to Securing Power Apps

Step 1: *Define User Roles and Permissions*

Before sharing your app, decide who needs access and what they should be able to do.

1. Open **Power Apps Studio** and navigate to **Settings**.
2. Select **Users and Permissions** from the menu.
3. Assign roles such as **Owner, Contributor, or User** based on access needs.
4. Save changes and notify users about their access levels.

Step 2: Enable Row-Level Security (RLS) in Dataverse

1. Open **Microsoft Dataverse** and navigate to **Tables**.
2. Select the table containing sensitive data.
3. Click **Manage Permissions** and choose **Row-Level Security**.
4. Define access rules so that only certain users or groups can view or edit specific records.
5. Save and test the security settings to ensure they work correctly.

Step 3: Implement Multi-Factor Authentication (MFA)

1. Open **Microsoft Entra ID (Azure Active Directory)** in the Microsoft portal.
2. Navigate to **Security > Authentication Methods**.
3. Enable **Multi-Factor Authentication (MFA)** for all Power Apps users.
4. Set up authentication options like SMS codes, authentication apps, or biometric verification.

Step 4: Limit App Sharing and Access

1. Open your **Power App** and click on **Share**.
2. Instead of sharing with "Everyone," manually **enter specific users or security groups**.
3. Set access permissions as **View-Only or Edit**, depending on the

user's role.

4. Regularly review access lists and remove users who no longer need access.

Step 5: Monitor Security Logs and Activity

1. Go to **Microsoft Power Platform Admin Center**.
2. Navigate to **Audit Logs** under **Security & Compliance**.
3. Check for any unusual login attempts, failed access attempts, or suspicious activities.
4. Set up alerts for **unauthorized access attempts** to quickly respond to potential threats.

9.2 Managing User Roles and Permissions

Security is not just about protecting data; it is about ensuring that the right people have the right level of access. In Power Apps, **managing user roles and permissions** is essential to maintain control over who can view, edit, or manage an application. Without proper role management, unauthorized users might access sensitive data, modify critical settings, or even disrupt operations.

1. Understanding User Roles in Power Apps

Power Apps provides a structured way to control access by defining **user roles**. Each role comes with specific permissions, ensuring that every user only has access to the features they need.

1.1 Why Role-Based Access Matters

- **Prevents unauthorized access** – Ensures that only authorized individuals can view or edit data.
- **Improves security** – Limits exposure of sensitive information to those who truly need it.
- **Enhances efficiency** – Users only see relevant tools and features, reducing confusion and errors.
- **Supports compliance** – Helps organizations meet data protection regulations by enforcing strict access rules.

1.2 Common User Roles in Power Apps

Power Apps classifies users into different roles based on their responsibilities. Below are the most commonly used roles:

- **Owner** – Has full control over the app, including editing, deleting, sharing, and managing permissions.
- **Contributor** – Can edit the app but does not have control over permissions or deletion.
- **User** – Can only use the app but cannot make changes or access administrative settings.
- **Guest** – Limited access, often granted to external users for temporary or restricted use.

Assigning the correct role ensures that **users only have the level of access they need** to perform their tasks, reducing security risks.

2. Assigning User Roles in Power Apps

Setting up user roles in Power Apps is a straightforward process. Follow these steps to ensure that permissions are correctly assigned.

Step 1: Open Power Apps

1. Log into **Power Apps** using your administrator account.
2. Navigate to the **Apps** section and select the app you want to manage.

Step 2: Access the Permissions Menu

1. Click on the **Settings** icon.
2. Select **Users and Permissions** from the menu.
3. Choose **Manage Users** to see the list of people who have access to the app.

Step 3: Assign Roles to Users

1. Click **Add Users** to invite new team members.
2. Enter their email addresses and select their **appropriate roles** (Owner, Contributor, User, or Guest).
3. Confirm by clicking **Save** to apply the changes.

Step 4: Review and Modify Roles Regularly

1. Periodically check user roles to ensure access levels remain appropriate.
2. Remove users who no longer need access or adjust their permissions as their responsibilities change.

213

By following these steps, administrators can effectively **control who can access and modify Power Apps applications**, preventing unauthorized use.

3. Managing Permissions for Data Access

User roles determine what actions someone can take within Power Apps, but **permissions control data visibility and access**. Ensuring the right permissions are in place is crucial for protecting sensitive information.

3.1 Setting Up Table-Level Security in Dataverse

If your Power App is connected to **Dataverse**, you can set permissions at the **table level** to restrict access to stored data.

1. Open **Dataverse** from the Power Platform Admin Center.
2. Click on **Tables** and select the table containing sensitive data.
3. Navigate to **Permissions** and define the level of access:

- **Full Control** – Users can view, edit, delete, and share records.
- **Read-Only** – Users can view records but cannot modify them.
- **Edit Access** – Users can change records but not delete them.
- **Restricted Access** – Users can only see specific data assigned to them.

1. Save changes and test the permissions by logging in as a restricted user.

3.2 Using Row-Level Security (RLS) for Precise Control

Row-Level Security (RLS) allows you to restrict access to individual records, ensuring that **users only see data relevant to their role**.

1. Open **Dataverse Security Settings**.
2. Select the table where you want to apply row-level restrictions.
3. Define security filters to specify which records users can access based on their role.
4. Apply and test the settings by logging in with different user accounts.

This ensures that **confidential information stays protected** while allowing necessary access for daily operations.

9.3 Setting Up Security for Data Sources

Data is the heart of any application, and protecting it is not just a necessity—it's a responsibility. Without proper security measures, sensitive information can fall into the wrong hands, leading to data breaches, financial loss, and even legal consequences. In Power Apps, **securing data sources** ensures that only authorized users can access, modify, or share information.

1. Understanding Data Security in Power Apps

Before setting up security, it's important to understand how Power Apps interacts with data. When an app connects to a **data source**, it acts as a bridge, retrieving and displaying data based on permissions. However, if access controls are weak, **users might gain unintended access** to confidential information.

Key security principles to follow:

- Restrict access to **only those who need it**
- Apply **role-based security** to define who can read, edit, or delete data
- Use **authentication methods** to verify user identity
- Encrypt data to prevent **unauthorized tampering**

Now, let's dive into the step-by-step process of securing different data sources.

2. Securing Dataverse Data

Microsoft Dataverse is a common data source for Power Apps, storing structured information like customer records, financial data, and business processes. To protect Dataverse data, follow these security measures:

Step 1: Assign Security Roles

1. Open **Power Platform Admin Center**.
2. Navigate to **Dataverse** and select your environment.
3. Click on **Security Roles** and review the existing roles.
4. Assign users to roles with appropriate permissions (e.g., Read-

Only, Editor, Administrator).

5. Save changes to apply the security settings.

Step 2: Set Up Table-Level Security

1. In **Dataverse**, select the table containing sensitive data.
2. Click on **Table Permissions** and choose access levels:

- **Full Control** – Users can read, edit, delete, and share records.
- **Read-Only** – Users can view records but not make changes.
- **Edit Access** – Users can modify records but not delete them.
- **Restricted Access** – Users can only access specific data assigned to them.

1. Apply the settings and test access with different user roles.

Step 3: Enable Row-Level Security (RLS)

If you need more control, **Row-Level Security (RLS)** allows you to **restrict individual records** to specific users or groups.

1. Go to **Dataverse Security Settings**.
2. Select the table where RLS is required.
3. Define **security filters** to limit access based on user roles.
4. Save and test by logging in as different users to verify restrictions.

3. Securing SharePoint as a Data Source

Many Power Apps use **SharePoint lists and libraries** to store information. If left unprotected, sensitive files can be accessed by unauthorized users. Here's how to secure SharePoint as a data source:

217

Step 1: Restrict SharePoint Permissions

1. Open **SharePoint** and navigate to the list or library.
2. Click on **Settings** > **Permissions for this list**.
3. Remove **inherited permissions** if needed.
4. Assign roles:

- **Full Control** – Only for administrators.
- **Edit** – For those who need to modify data.
- **Read-Only** – For users who only need to view data.
- **Restricted** – Limit access to specific users or groups.

1. Click **Save** to apply the settings.

Step 2: Enable Multi-Factor Authentication (MFA)

Adding an extra layer of security helps prevent unauthorized logins.

1. Go to **Microsoft Entra ID (formerly Azure Active Directory)**.
2. Click on **Security** > **Multi-Factor Authentication**.
3. Enforce MFA for all users accessing SharePoint data.
4. Save settings to activate protection.

4. Securing SQL Databases in Power Apps

If your Power App connects to an **SQL database**, proper security settings prevent unauthorized users from accessing sensitive data. Follow these steps:

Step 1: Use Role-Based Security in SQL

1. Open **SQL Server Management Studio (SSMS)**.
2. Select the database used in Power Apps.
3. Go to **Security** > **Users** and create roles:

- **Admin** – Full access to all tables.
- **Editor** – Can update records but not delete them.
- **Viewer** – Can only read data, no modifications allowed.

1. Assign users to appropriate roles.

Step 2: Restrict Access with Firewalls

1. Open **Azure SQL Database Settings** (if using cloud storage).
2. Click on **Networking** > **Firewall Rules**.
3. Allow access only from **trusted devices and networks**.
4. Disable public access if possible.

Step 3: Encrypt Data for Extra Security

1. Enable **Transparent Data Encryption (TDE)** in SQL.
2. Use **Always Encrypted** to protect sensitive columns like credit card numbers.
3. Save settings and verify encryption is active.

5. Protecting External APIs and Third-Party Data Sources

Power Apps can also **connect to external APIs** for retrieving and sending data. If these APIs are not secured, attackers can exploit them.

Step 1: Use API Authentication Methods

1. Instead of open access, require **OAuth 2.0** or API keys for authentication.
2. Store API keys securely using **Azure Key Vault**.
3. Restrict API calls to **trusted IP addresses**.

Step 2: Set API Access Limits

1. In API settings, define rate limits to prevent excessive requests.
2. Monitor API usage and **block suspicious activity**.

Step 3: Encrypt API Data in Transit

1. Ensure the API uses **HTTPS (SSL/TLS encryption)** to protect data.
2. Reject all **unsecured HTTP requests** to prevent data exposure.

9.4 Role-Based Access Control (RBAC) in Power Apps

Security is the foundation of any successful application. It ensures that users only access the data and features necessary for their roles, preventing unauthorized changes and protecting sensitive information. One of the most effective ways to manage security in **Power Apps** is through **Role-Based Access Control (RBAC)**.

RBAC helps **control permissions efficiently**, ensuring that each user has the right level of access based on their role within the organization. This method prevents unnecessary exposure of critical data and ensures smooth, structured operations within an application.

1. Understanding Role-Based Access Control (RBAC)

RBAC is a security model that **assigns permissions to users based on their job responsibilities** rather than granting unrestricted access to everyone. Instead of giving all users the same level of control, RBAC **limits permissions** based on predefined roles.

For example:

- **Administrator** – Has full access to create, edit, delete, and manage all data and settings.
- **Manager** – Can approve changes, modify specific records, but cannot delete sensitive data.
- **Employee** – Can view records and update limited information but cannot make structural changes.
- **Guest** – Has read-only access and cannot modify any records.

By defining roles, **organizations can ensure that employees only interact with the data and functions relevant to their work**, reducing security risks and data mishandling.

2. How RBAC Works in Power Apps

In **Power Apps**, RBAC functions by integrating **Microsoft Dataverse security roles, SharePoint permissions, or external authentication providers** like **Azure Active Directory (Microsoft Entra ID)**. Permissions are assigned at different levels to control:

- **Who can access the application**
- **What data they can view or modify**
- **Which actions they are allowed to perform**

RBAC can be implemented using **Dataverse Security Roles, SharePoint Role Assignments, or Custom Power Automate Flows** to restrict access based on user identity.

3. Implementing RBAC in Power Apps (Step-by-Step Guide)

Step 1: Identify User Roles and Access Needs

Before setting up RBAC, outline the different user roles and their required access levels. Consider:

- Who needs **full control** over the app?
- Which users should only have **limited access**?
- Are there any roles that require **read-only permissions**?
- Should certain users be restricted from **viewing specific data**?

Creating a **clear role structure** will help you apply security settings effectively.

Step 2: Implement Role-Based Security in Microsoft Dataverse

If your Power App is connected to **Dataverse**, use built-in security roles to control access:

1. Open **Power Platform Admin Center**.
2. Navigate to **Dataverse** and select your environment.
3. Click on **Security Roles** and choose **Create a New Role** or modify an existing one.
4. Define access levels for each role:

- **Full Control** (Admins)
- **Modify Data** (Managers)
- **Read-Only Access** (Employees)

1. Assign users to the roles based on their responsibilities.
2. Click **Save and Apply** to activate the security settings.

By assigning roles in Dataverse, **you ensure that only authorized users can perform specific actions**, reducing the risk of data breaches or accidental modifications.

Step 3: Secure SharePoint Data with Role-Based Permissions

If your Power App **pulls data from SharePoint**, you can restrict access using SharePoint security settings:

1. Open **SharePoint** and go to the document library or list used in

Power Apps.

2. Click on **Settings** > **Permissions for this List/Library**.
3. Remove inherited permissions (if necessary) to apply custom security settings.
4. Assign user roles:

- **Owners** – Full access to edit and manage permissions.
- **Members** – Can add and modify data but cannot delete important files.
- **Visitors** – Read-only access.

1. Click **Save Changes** to apply the role-based security settings.

Using SharePoint's built-in role management, **you can ensure that sensitive business documents remain protected while allowing employees to collaborate effectively**.

Step 4: Configure RBAC in Power Automate (For Advanced Security Control)

For applications requiring **custom workflows**, Power Automate can be used to control access dynamically:

1. Open **Power Automate** and create a **new flow**.
2. Use **Condition Logic** to check the user's role before executing actions.
3. Define rules such as:

- If **User Role = Manager**, allow **record updates**.
- If **User Role = Employee**, allow **only data entry**.
- If **User Role = Guest**, allow **view access but restrict editing**.

1. Test the workflow to ensure it properly restricts actions based on user roles.
2. Click **Save and Activate** to enable role-based automation.

This approach **adds an extra layer of control**, ensuring that workflows execute only when authorized users initiate them.

4. Best Practices for Using RBAC in Power Apps

To maximize security and efficiency, follow these best practices:

1. Apply the Principle of Least Privilege (PoLP)

Only grant users **the minimum level of access needed** to perform their tasks. Avoid assigning full control unless absolutely necessary.

2. Regularly Review and Update Roles

As **business needs evolve**, user roles may need adjustments. Periodically **audit security settings** to ensure they align with current responsibilities.

3. Implement Multi-Factor Authentication (MFA)

Adding **MFA** ensures that users must verify their identity before accessing sensitive data, reducing security risks.

4. Monitor Access Logs

Use **Microsoft Entra ID (Azure AD) logs** to track login activity and detect any unauthorized access attempts.

5. Protect API and External Data Access

If your Power App connects to external services, **use API authentication methods** such as OAuth or API tokens to prevent unauthorized access.

5. The Impact of Role-Based Access Control

Implementing **RBAC in Power Apps** brings numerous benefits, including:

- **Stronger Security** – Prevents unauthorized users from modifying or accessing critical data.
- **Better Compliance** – Ensures organizations meet security regulations and industry standards.
- **Improved Efficiency** – Employees can focus on tasks relevant to their roles without unnecessary access distractions.
- **Reduced Errors** – Minimizes accidental changes that could lead to data loss or corruption.

By following a structured **role-based security model**, you create a **safe, well-organized system** where each user has the exact level of control needed—no more, no less.

9.5 Auditing and Compliance

Security is not just about protecting data; it's about maintaining trust. Every organization needs a **reliable system** to track activities, ensure compliance with regulations, and safeguard sensitive information from unauthorized access or misuse. This is where **auditing and compliance** play a crucial role in **Power Apps**.

Auditing helps organizations **monitor user actions**, detect suspicious activities, and maintain records for future reference. Compliance ensures that business applications **adhere to legal and industry standards**, preventing penalties and reputational damage.

1. Understanding Auditing in Power Apps

Auditing refers to the process of **tracking and recording user activities within an application**. It helps administrators:

- **Identify unauthorized access or changes**
- **Monitor data usage and modifications**
- **Ensure accountability by keeping a record of user actions**
- **Detect and resolve security breaches before they cause damage**

Audit logs **act as a digital footprint**, capturing critical information such as **who accessed the app, what actions were performed, and when changes were made**.

2. The Importance of Compliance

Compliance ensures that an application follows **legal, regulatory, and industry standards**. Depending on the organization and the nature of the data being handled, compliance may involve:

- **Data Protection Laws** (such as GDPR, HIPAA, or CCPA)
- **Industry-Specific Regulations** (such as finance, healthcare, or government policies)
- **Internal Company Policies** (established rules for data security and governance)

Failing to meet compliance standards **can result in financial penalties, legal consequences, and a loss of customer trust**. That's why organizations must implement **strong auditing practices to maintain compliance and protect user data**.

3. Setting Up Auditing in Power Apps (Step-by-Step Guide)

Step 1: Enable Auditing in Microsoft Dataverse

If your Power App is built using **Dataverse**, you can enable auditing to track user activities.

1. Open **Power Platform Admin Center**.
2. Navigate to **Environments** and select the environment where your Power App is deployed.
3. Click on **Settings**, then go to **Auditing** under **Data Management**.
4. Enable **Audit Logging** and specify the data types to be tracked:

228

- **User logins and access attempts**
- **Data creation, updates, and deletions**
- **Changes to security settings**

1. Click **Save** to activate auditing.

Once enabled, **audit logs automatically record user actions**, allowing administrators to **review activity history and investigate any issues**.

Step 2: Monitor User Activities with Power Automate

For more control over **audit tracking**, Power Automate can be used to **send alerts** when suspicious activities occur.

1. Open **Power Automate** and create a **new flow**.
2. Select **Dataverse as the trigger** and choose "When a record is created, updated, or deleted."
3. Define **conditions** to monitor specific activities (e.g., unauthorized data deletions).
4. Set up **email notifications** or log entries when unusual actions occur.
5. Test the flow and activate it to start tracking user behavior automatically.

This method allows organizations to **proactively detect security issues** before they escalate into serious threats.

Step 3: Review Audit Logs Regularly

Audit logs provide valuable insights, but they are only useful if they are reviewed consistently.

1. Open **Power Platform Admin Center** and navigate to **Audit Logs**.
2. Filter records based on **date, user activity, or specific actions**.
3. Look for **suspicious patterns**, such as repeated failed login attempts or unauthorized data access.
4. Export logs for deeper analysis or compliance reporting.
5. Investigate and resolve any security concerns immediately.

Regularly checking audit logs helps **strengthen security measures** and ensures that the application remains **compliant with industry regulations**.

4. Ensuring Compliance in Power Apps

1. Data Security Policies

Establish clear security policies, such as **who can access sensitive data and under what conditions**. Use **role-based access control (RBAC)** to limit unnecessary data exposure.

2. Implement Data Retention Policies

Some regulations require businesses to store records for a specific period. Define **data retention and deletion rules** to comply with legal requirements.

3. Encrypt Sensitive Information

Use **Microsoft Dataverse encryption** to protect confidential data. Ensure that sensitive information is stored securely and cannot be accessed by unauthorized users.

4. Enable Multi-Factor Authentication (MFA)

Requiring users to verify their identity with **MFA** before accessing critical data prevents **unauthorized logins** and strengthens security.

5. Regular Security Audits

Conduct periodic **security assessments** to identify vulnerabilities and ensure compliance. Review **audit logs, permissions, and security configurations** to maintain a safe environment.

5. Benefits of Auditing and Compliance in Power Apps

- **Enhanced Security** – Protects against unauthorized access and data breaches.
- **Regulatory Compliance** – Ensures adherence to laws and industry standards, preventing legal issues.
- **Improved Accountability** – Tracks user actions, reducing the risk of insider threats or accidental errors.
- **Quick Issue Resolution** – Helps detect and address security risks before they become major problems.

Chapter 10: Performance Optimization

10.1 Best Practices for Power Apps Performance

A well-designed Power App is more than just visually appealing—it should be **fast, efficient, and responsive**. No one wants to use an application that lags, crashes, or takes too long to load. Slow performance can frustrate users, reduce productivity, and even impact business operations. That's why optimizing your Power App is essential to ensure a **seamless user experience**.

Performance optimization is not just about fixing issues after they arise; it's about **building an app with efficiency in mind from the very beginning**. By following **best practices**, you can make sure your app runs smoothly, loads quickly, and performs well under different conditions.

1. Optimize Data Sources for Faster Loading

Data is at the heart of any Power App, but **inefficient data management can slow everything down**. The way your app **fetches, processes, and displays data** significantly affects its performance.

How to Optimize Data Sources:

1. **Use Delegation for Large Data Sets**

   • When working with **large amounts of data**, always use **delegation-friendly functions** like Filter(), Sort(), and Search().
   • Avoid non-delegable functions like ForAll(), as they process data on the device instead of the server, slowing things down.

1. **Limit the Number of Data Calls**

   • Avoid **pulling unnecessary data** by filtering results before loading them.
   • Use queries that **fetch only the data you need**, rather than loading an entire table.

1. **Use Collections Wisely**

   • **Collections** are useful for storing temporary data, but excessive use can slow down performance.
   • Instead of storing large datasets in collections, try to retrieve data only when needed.

1. **Optimize Data Sources in Dataverse**

- If using **Dataverse**, enable indexing on frequently searched columns.
- Reduce the number of **lookup fields and relationships** to avoid complex queries.

2. Reduce App Load Time

A slow-loading app discourages users and creates a poor experience. **Reducing the time it takes to open an app can make a big difference**.

How to Speed Up App Loading:

1. **Load Only Essential Data on Start**

- Instead of loading all data immediately, **load only what is necessary for the first screen**.
- Use **OnVisible** or **On Select** events to fetch additional data when required.

1. **Optimize On Start Actions**

- Many apps run multiple commands in **App.On Start**, which can cause delays.
- Move non-critical actions to other parts of the app to **prevent slow startup times**.

1. **Use Global Variables and Context Variables Efficiently**

- Avoid excessive use of **global variables**, as they can slow performance.

- Instead, use **context variables** or **collections** to store frequently accessed values.

3. Improve Screen Navigation Speed

Navigating between screens should be **instant and smooth**. A slow transition between screens **affects user experience and workflow efficiency**.

How to Improve Screen Navigation:

1. **Minimize the Number of Controls Per Screen**

- Too many controls on a single screen **increase rendering time**.
- Keep only **essential elements** and consider using pop-ups or multiple screens.

1. **Use Loading Indicators**

- If a screen needs time to load data, **show a loading spinner** to keep users informed.
- This prevents users from thinking the app is unresponsive.

1. **Preload Data for Frequently Used Screens**

- If a user frequently navigates between two screens, **store some data in memory** for faster access.
- This reduces **repetitive data fetch requests**.

4. Optimize Form Performance

Forms are commonly used for **data entry and user input**, but they can slow down an app if not optimized properly.

How to Make Forms Run Faster:

1. **Use Edit Forms Instead of Individual Input Fields**

- Instead of creating multiple text inputs, use **Edit Forms** to handle data more efficiently.
- This reduces **the number of controls** and improves app performance.

1. **Limit the Number of Fields Per Form**

- Too many fields slow down performance. Only include **essential input fields**.
- If necessary, break the form into **multiple steps or sections**.

1. **Disable Unused Form Features**

- If a form does not need attachments, turn off **unnecessary features** to speed up processing.

5. Optimize Power Automate Flows for Better Performance

Power Automate is often used **alongside Power Apps** for automation, but poorly designed flows **can delay app execution**.

How to Optimize Power Automate Flows:

1. **Reduce the Number of Flow Runs**

- Avoid triggering unnecessary flows.
- Use **conditional logic** to ensure flows **only run when needed**.

1. **Use Parallel Branching for Faster Execution**

- Instead of running actions **one by one**, use parallel branches to **execute multiple tasks simultaneously**.

1. **Limit API Calls and External Data Requests**

- Repeated calls to external APIs or databases **increase response time**.
- If possible, cache data and use stored values.

10.2 Optimizing Data Calls and Load Times

A fast and responsive app isn't just a luxury—it's a necessity. No one wants to wait endlessly for a page to load or an action to complete. Slow data calls and long load times can frustrate users, disrupt workflow, and reduce efficiency. Whether you're building an internal business tool or a customer-facing application, **optimization is key to creating a smooth experience**.

1. Minimize Data Calls for Better Speed

Every time your app fetches data, it consumes resources. If data calls are inefficient, they **slow down performance and increase load times**. Reducing unnecessary requests can make a huge difference.

How to Minimize Data Calls:

1. **Fetch Only What You Need**

- Avoid retrieving entire tables when you only need **a few columns or rows**.
- Use filtering and sorting techniques to **retrieve relevant data only**.

1. **Use Delegation-Friendly Queries**

- Power Apps processes large datasets more efficiently **when delegation is enabled**.
- Functions like Filter(), Sort(), and Search() work best with **delegable data sources**.

238

1. **Limit Refreshing of Data Sources**

- Avoid refreshing the entire dataset **every time a user interacts with the app**.
- Instead, **refresh only when data changes** or when it's absolutely necessary.

1. **Reduce On-Demand API Calls**

- If your app depends on external APIs, **minimize the number of requests**.
- Store retrieved data locally in **variables or collections** to avoid repetitive calls.

2. Optimize Data Loading for Faster App Performance

A slow-loading app can drive users away. Instead of fetching everything at once, use **efficient data-loading techniques** to ensure a smooth experience.

How to Optimize Data Loading:

1. **Load Data in the Background**

- Instead of making users wait for everything to load, **use asynchronous loading**.
- Fetch data in the background and display placeholders or progress indicators.

1. **Preload Frequently Used Data**

- If some data is **constantly required**, preload it when the app starts.
- Store it in **collections or global variables** to avoid repeated data calls.

1. **Lazy Loading for Large Data Sets**

- Instead of loading everything at once, use **lazy loading** to fetch data **as needed**.
- For example, **load only the first 50 records** and fetch more when scrolling.

1. **Cache Data for Faster Access**

- Store recently used data **in local memory** to reduce repeated queries.
- This speeds up performance, especially when dealing with **static or rarely changing data**.

3. Reduce Screen Load Times with Smart Design

The design of your app **affects its speed**. Too many controls, excessive queries, or inefficient functions can slow things down.

How to Reduce Screen Load Time:

1. **Minimize the Number of Controls**

- Each control adds to **rendering time**, so keep only essential elements.
- If possible, **combine multiple controls** into a single gallery or

container.

1. Use Galleries Instead of Individual Controls

- Instead of displaying multiple labels, **use a gallery** to bind data dynamically.
- This **reduces rendering load** and improves responsiveness.

1. Optimize Images and Media

- Large images and videos **increase load time**.
- Compress media files or **use lower-resolution versions** to speed up performance.

4. Improve Query Efficiency for Faster Data Retrieval

Poorly designed queries can **cause delays** and put unnecessary load on your database. Optimizing how your app **queries and retrieves data** can significantly improve speed.

How to Improve Query Performance:

1. Use Indexed Columns in Dataverse or SharePoint

- Indexed columns make searching and filtering much faster.
- If you're using **Dataverse, SQL, or SharePoint**, enable indexing on frequently searched fields.

1. Use Filter and Sort Before Collecting Data

- Instead of fetching all records and then filtering, apply filters

before retrieving data.

- This reduces the **number of records processed at once**.

1. **Batch Process Data Updates**

- If your app needs to update multiple records, use **batch processing** instead of updating one by one.
- This reduces **network traffic and improves response time**.

1. **Optimize Lookup Fields**

- Too many lookup fields can slow down queries.
- Use **text or choice fields** instead when possible to speed up data retrieval.

10.3 Troubleshooting Common Performance Issues

No one wants to use a slow, unresponsive app. When an application takes too long to load or frequently crashes, users quickly become frustrated. Performance issues can turn a great idea into a frustrating experience, reducing productivity and making tasks more difficult than they should be.

To ensure your Power App runs smoothly, you must **identify, diagnose, and resolve performance problems efficiently**.

1. Identifying Performance Bottlenecks

Before fixing an issue, you need to **find out what's causing the slowdown**. Performance problems can stem from inefficient data handling, too many controls, excessive queries, or poor design choices.

How to Identify the Root Cause:

1. **Check App Load Times**

- If your app takes too long to open, **examine what's loading at startup**.
- Reduce the number of **preloaded data sources or unnecessary screens**.

1. **Use Power Apps Monitor**

- The **Monitor tool** tracks data calls, errors, and response times.
- Look for slow-loading queries or excessive API calls.

1. **Analyze Network and Data Queries**

- Large datasets or multiple **simultaneous queries** can cause delays.
- Test if reducing the number of **data requests** improves speed.

1. **Test on Different Devices**

- Performance may vary based on **device type, internet speed, or browser**.
- If it runs well on a computer but lags on mobile, **optimize for**

243

mobile use.

1. **Check Memory and CPU Usage**

- If your app frequently **freezes or crashes**, it may be **using too much memory**.
- Reducing unnecessary **animations, controls, or background processes** can help.

2. Fixing Slow Data Retrieval

One of the most common issues in Power Apps is **slow data loading**. Fetching large datasets without proper filtering can **overload the system**, making the app sluggish.

Solutions to Speed Up Data Retrieval:

1. **Reduce Data Calls**

- Instead of retrieving entire datasets, **load only the necessary records**.
- Use Filter(), Search(), and Sort() functions **before** fetching data.

1. **Use Delegation for Large Data Sources**

- Ensure queries are **delegable** so Power Apps **processes data on the server**, not the device.
- Work with **delegable functions** to avoid performance issues when handling **large lists or tables**.

1. **Cache Frequently Used Data**

244

- Store static or repeated data in **global variables or collections**.
- This **reduces the need for repeated queries** and speeds up performance.

1. **Optimize Lookup Fields**

- Too many lookup fields slow down queries.
- Replace lookup fields with **text or choice fields** whenever possible.

3. Solving App Freezing and Crashes

If your app frequently **crashes or becomes unresponsive**, it might be handling too many tasks at once. Poorly optimized controls, excessive data calls, and **unnecessary background processes** can cause instability.

Ways to Fix Freezing and Crashes:

1. **Reduce the Number of Controls**

- Each control adds to the app's processing load.
- Combine multiple controls **into galleries or containers** for better efficiency.

1. **Avoid Unnecessary Data Refreshes**

- Refreshing a dataset **every few seconds** puts unnecessary strain on the app.
- Instead, update data **only when changes occur** or on user request.

1. **Optimize Large Forms and Screens**

- Large forms with **multiple input fields** can slow things down.
- Split long forms into **multiple steps** or use a **tabbed interface**.

1. **Limit Background Processes**

- Too many background calculations **consume memory and slow down performance**.
- Use timers **only when necessary** and minimize unnecessary triggers.

4. Improving Slow Navigation Between Screens

If switching between screens takes too long, it affects the **flow and usability** of the app. Users expect quick transitions, and **delays can be frustrating**.

Ways to Improve Navigation Speed:

1. **Preload Data in the Background**

- Instead of fetching data **every time a user switches screens**, preload important information at the start.
- Store it in **collections or local variables** for faster access.

1. **Use On Visible Instead of On Select**

- Instead of calling data functions when a button is clicked (On Select), fetch data when a screen **becomes visible (On Visible)**.
- This reduces lag when navigating.

246

1. **Minimize Screen Elements**

- Too many controls on a single screen slow down rendering.
- Use galleries, containers, and **dynamic visibility** to show only **what's needed**.

5. Fixing Slow Search and Filtering

If searching for records takes too long, it could be due to **poorly optimized queries or a lack of delegation**. A slow search function **frustrates users and reduces productivity**.

Steps to Optimize Search Performance:

1. **Use Indexed Columns in Data Sources**

- Indexed columns in **Dataverse, SQL, or SharePoint** allow **faster searches**.
- Applying indexing to frequently searched fields can **reduce search time significantly**.

1. **Filter Data Before Searching**

- Instead of searching through **all records**, apply filters to **reduce the dataset first**.
- For example, **filter by date range before searching for a name**.

1. **Use Delegable Search Functions**

- Ensure search queries are **delegable** so they are processed on the **server side**, not within Power Apps.

- Functions like Search(), LookUp(), and StartsWith() work best with **delegable data sources**.

1. **Limit the Number of Search Results**

- Display only the **first 50 or 100 results,** then load more **as needed**.
- This prevents unnecessary **strain on the system**.

6. Monitoring and Preventing Future Issues

After resolving performance issues, **regular monitoring** helps prevent new problems from arising.

How to Keep Your App Running Smoothly:

1. **Use Power Apps Performance Insights**

- Review **load times, errors, and query execution speeds**.
- Fix slow components **before they become major issues**.

1. **Test with Different Users and Devices**

- Performance can vary based on **network conditions, devices, and user roles**.
- Regular testing **helps identify weaknesses**.

1. **Keep the App Updated**

- Power Apps constantly evolves with **new optimizations and improvements**.

- Updating your app **ensures compatibility with the latest performance enhancements**.

1. **Train Users on Best Practices**

- Users should know **how to avoid unnecessary data refreshes** or **manage searches efficiently**.
- A well-informed user base **reduces system overload**.

10.4 Tips for Building Scalable Apps for Large User Groups

Creating an app that performs well for a few users is one thing, but ensuring it runs smoothly for **hundreds or even thousands** is an entirely different challenge. As the number of users grows, the strain on the system increases, and without proper planning, the app may slow down, crash, or become unmanageable.

Scalability is about **building an app that can handle increasing users and data without compromising performance**. If designed well, an app will **grow effortlessly** alongside the business, ensuring a seamless experience for everyone.

1. Choose the Right Data Source for Scalability

The backbone of any app is **how it stores and manages data**. If an app is expected to support a large user base, selecting the **right data source** is crucial.

How to Ensure Your Data Source Can Handle Growth:

1. **Use Dataverse for Enterprise-Scale Apps**

- Unlike SharePoint or Excel, **Dataverse** is designed for **highperformance apps.**
- It can handle **large datasets, relationships, and security** more efficiently.

1. **Limit the Use of SharePoint for Large Data Loads**

- SharePoint works well for **smaller apps**, but performance declines with **thousands of records.**
- For anything beyond **5,000 records**, consider **Dataverse, SQL Server, or Azure.**

1. **Optimize SQL Databases for Fast Queries**

- If using SQL, ensure tables have **indexed columns** to **speed up searches.**
- Use stored procedures for **complex calculations**, reducing processing load on the app.

2. Minimize Data Load for Faster Performance

Fetching large amounts of data at once **slows down the app and affects usability.** When multiple users are accessing the system simultaneously, optimizing how data is retrieved is essential.

How to Reduce Data Load Without Losing Important Information:

1. **Load Only What's Needed**

- Instead of retrieving an entire dataset, fetch only **the necessary fields and records**.
- Use Filter(), LookUp(), and Sort() functions to **narrow down data** before retrieving it.

1. **Use Collections for Frequently Used Data**

- Store static or frequently accessed information in **collections** to avoid repeated database calls.
- For example, **user roles, dropdown lists, or reference data** can be cached at app startup.

1. **Use Pagination Instead of Loading All Data**

- Instead of displaying **thousands of records at once**, show **only a small batch** (e.g., 50 at a time).
- Load more results only **when the user scrolls or requests additional data**.

1. **Filter Data on the Server, Not the App**

- **Delegation** allows filtering and searching **directly in the data source**, improving speed.
- Avoid non-delegable functions like Left(), Right(), or Mid() on large datasets.

3. Efficiently Manage User Access and Security

As more users join the app, **security and access control become critical**. A scalable app must balance **performance with user permissions** to ensure data integrity and privacy.

Best Practices for Managing Users Securely:

1. **Implement Role-Based Security**

- Define **different access levels** for **admins, managers, and general users**.
- Use **Dataverse security roles** or SharePoint permissions to control access.

1. **Limit Data Visibility with Security Filters**

- Instead of **loading all user data**, show only what's relevant to each person.
- Use User().Email or User().FullName to filter records **based on login credentials**.

1. **Avoid Storing Sensitive Information in the App**

- Store sensitive data in **secure locations like Dataverse or Azure**, not in collections.
- Encrypt important information where necessary.

1. **Monitor User Activity for Performance Insights**

- Use **Power Platform Analytics** to track user behavior and identify potential bottlenecks.

- If certain actions slow down the app, **optimize queries or adjust permissions** accordingly.

4. Optimize App Design for Speed and Usability

A scalable app should not only handle many users but also **provide a smooth experience for each one**. Poor design choices can make even the most powerful app feel slow and inefficient.

Steps to Improve App Performance and Usability:

1. **Reduce the Number of Controls**

- Every control added to a screen **increases the load time**.
- Use **galleries, tabbed interfaces, and collapsible sections** to organize content efficiently.

1. **Use Components for Repeated Elements**

- Instead of **copying and pasting buttons or menus** across screens, create reusable components.
- This reduces maintenance time and **improves loading speed**.

1. **Limit the Use of Timers and Auto-Refresh**

- Frequent auto-refreshing drains resources.
- Instead, update data **only when necessary** or based on user actions.

1. **Use Simple, Clean Navigation**

- Avoid cluttering screens with **too many options or unnecessary details**.
- Implement a **consistent menu structure** for easy navigation.

5. Plan for Growth and Future Enhancements

A scalable app should be designed **not just for today's needs but for future expansion**. As user demand increases, the app should be able to adapt without major overhauls.

How to Future-Proof Your App:

1. **Use Modular Design**

- Break the app into **reusable components and sections** so new features can be added easily.
- Keep the **core functions separate** from temporary features.

1. **Monitor Performance Regularly**

- Keep track of **app response times, data usage, and server load**.
- Optimize processes based on **real-time user feedback and analytics**.

1. **Keep the Codebase Clean and Documented**

- Clearly label functions, variables, and screens to **make future updates easier**.
- Write detailed notes on **how the app is structured** to help future developers.

1. **Stay Updated with Power Apps Improvements**

- Microsoft frequently releases **new features and performance enhancements**.
- Regularly update the app to **take advantage of the latest optimizations**.

10.5 Analyzing App Performance Using Monitoring Tools

Building a high-performing app is not just about design and development; it's about **ensuring the app runs smoothly over time**. Even the most well-structured apps can experience **slowdowns, unexpected errors, or inefficiencies** when used by a large number of people. This is where **monitoring tools** come into play.

Monitoring tools **help identify performance bottlenecks, track app usage, and detect issues before they affect users**. By continuously analyzing how the app is performing, adjustments can be made **to improve speed, reduce errors, and optimize the user experience**.

1. Why Monitoring App Performance is Important

Without proper monitoring, it's difficult to **pinpoint what's causing slow performance**. Sometimes an app may seem to work fine during testing, but as more users interact with it, **issues start appearing**.

Common Problems That Performance Monitoring Helps Solve:

- **Slow loading times** when opening the app or navigating between screens.
- **Delayed responses** when clicking buttons or retrieving data.
- **High resource usage**, causing the app to freeze or crash.
- **Errors in data retrieval** due to broken connections or misconfigured formulas.
- **Unoptimized queries** that overload the system, making the app sluggish.

By using monitoring tools, these problems can be identified **before they affect users**, allowing you to make quick fixes and keep your app running smoothly.

2. Tools for Monitoring Power Apps Performance

Power Apps offers several built-in and external tools that help track **app speed, data usage, and error logs**. Knowing which tool to use for each scenario ensures a **proactive approach to performance optimization**.

Key Monitoring Tools and How to Use Them:

1. Monitor in Power Apps Studio

Purpose: Tracks real-time performance while testing the app.
  How to Use:

- Open the app in **Power Apps Studio**.
- Click on **Advanced Tools** > **Monitor**.

- Run the app and observe how different actions affect performance.
- Identify slow data calls, heavy screen loads, or errors in real-time.

Benefits:

- Detects **inefficient formulas and slow queries**.
- Helps optimize **database calls and screen transitions**.
- Provides **detailed logs for debugging issues quickly**.

2. Power Apps Analytics in the Power Platform Admin Center

Purpose: Provides usage insights and performance reports over time.
How to Use:

- Go to **Power Platform Admin Center**.
- Click on **Analytics > Power Apps**.
- Review reports on **app usage, load times, and error rates**.
- Identify **trends** that could indicate **performance degradation**.

Benefits:

- Helps track **which users are experiencing issues**.
- Identifies **frequent crashes or loading delays**.
- Provides **historical data to see performance trends over time**.

3. Performance Insights in App Checker

Purpose: Detects formula inefficiencies and delegation issues.
How to Use:

- Open the app in **Power Apps Studio**.

258

- Click on **App Checker** in the toolbar.
- Look for **warnings about delegation, slow queries, or missing references**.

Benefits:

- Ensures **data filtering is handled by the server (not the app)**.
- Highlights **heavy functions that slow down performance**.
- Suggests **alternative solutions for faster app execution**.

4. Microsoft Dataverse Analytics

Purpose: Monitors data transactions and system resource usage.
How to Use:

- Open **Power Platform Admin Center**.
- Navigate to **Analytics > Dataverse**.
- Check reports on **API calls, query execution time, and database load**.

Benefits:

- Helps optimize **database queries for faster response times**.
- Identifies **data sources that may be overloaded**.
- Provides insights into **how different entities are performing**.

5. Session Monitoring with Developer Tools (Google Chrome/F12)

Purpose: Identifies network issues and slow data calls.
   How to Use:

- Open **Google Chrome** (or Microsoft Edge).
- Press **F12** to open Developer Tools.
- Click on the **Network tab** and run the app.
- Look for **long response times in API calls** or **failed requests**.

Benefits:

- Shows **real-time delays in data retrieval**.
- Identifies **errors in API connections**.
- Helps debug **slow-loading pages or missing resources**.

3. How to Interpret Monitoring Data and Improve Performance

Simply collecting performance data isn't enough; it's essential to **analyze the information and take action**. Below are key areas to focus on when evaluating performance reports.

1. Identify Slow Data Calls and Optimize Queries

If a data call is taking too long:

- Reduce the number of records retrieved.
- Use **delegable functions** to let the server handle filtering.
- Store **frequently used data in collections** instead of fetching it

repeatedly.

2. Analyze Load Times and Improve Screen Transitions

If screens take a long time to load:

- Reduce the number of **controls and components** on each screen.
- Avoid complex formulas in the **On Visible** property (use **On Start** instead).
- Preload data in the background using **On Start variables**.

3. Reduce API Calls and Improve Connection Efficiency

If external API calls slow down the app:

- Batch multiple API requests together to reduce **network overhead**.
- Use caching where possible to avoid **repeated data requests**.
- Ensure APIs return **only the necessary data fields**.

4. Track User Behavior and Improve Navigation Flow

If users struggle with slow navigation:

- Monitor user session data to see where they get stuck.
- Simplify menus and optimize **button placements** for faster actions.
- Reduce unnecessary screens and keep navigation **intuitive and direct**.

5. Detect and Fix Errors Before They Affect Users

If errors frequently appear in logs:

- Review error messages in **Monitor and Power Platform Analytics**.
- Check data sources for **connection issues or missing references**.
- Ensure formulas are optimized and do not contain **circular dependencies**.

Chapter 11: Extending Power Apps Functionality

11.1 Using Microsoft Azure with Power Apps

Technology is constantly evolving, and so are the demands of modern applications. As businesses grow, so does the need for **more powerful, flexible, and scalable solutions**. While Power Apps offers incredible tools for building applications quickly, there comes a time when you need **more advanced features, deeper integrations, and better performance**. This is where **Microsoft Azure** becomes a game changer.

By integrating Power Apps with Microsoft Azure, you **unlock a world of possibilities**—from handling large amounts of data to adding artificial intelligence and automation. Whether you're looking to improve security, process data faster, or create complex workflows, Azure provides the tools to take your Power Apps to the next level.

1. Why Integrate Microsoft Azure with Power Apps?

Power Apps is designed to be simple and accessible, but sometimes, businesses need **more than just basic app-building capabilities**. Azure offers **cloud-based solutions that enhance Power Apps**, making them more **scalable, secure, and intelligent**.

Key Benefits of Using Azure with Power Apps:

- **Scalability:** Handle large datasets and complex processes without slowing down your app.
- **Advanced Security:** Protect sensitive data with enterprise-grade security features.
- **AI and Automation:** Use **Azure AI** and **Machine Learning** to make apps smarter.
- **Efficient Data Processing:** Improve performance by storing and analyzing data in **Azure SQL Database** or **Azure Data Lake**.
- **Powerful Integrations:** Connect Power Apps with **Azure Logic Apps, Functions, and API Management** to build advanced workflows.

By extending Power Apps with Azure, you ensure your applications remain **fast, efficient, and capable of handling large-scale business operations**.

2. Connecting Power Apps to Azure

Before using Azure services, you need to establish a **connection between Power Apps and Azure**. Fortunately, Microsoft provides seamless integration options that make this process straightforward.

Steps to Connect Power Apps with Azure:

Step 1: Choose the Right Azure Service

Azure offers various services, each designed for different needs. Before connecting, determine **which service best suits your app's requirements**:

- **Azure SQL Database:** Ideal for storing large volumes of structured data.
- **Azure Functions:** Great for running small code snippets in response to app events.
- **Azure Logic Apps:** Automates workflows across different systems.
- **Azure Cognitive Services:** Adds AI-powered features like speech recognition and sentiment analysis.

Step 2: Set Up an Azure Subscription

To access Azure services, you need an **Azure subscription**. If you don't have one:

- Visit **Microsoft Azure Portal** and sign up.
- Choose a **subscription plan** based on your needs.
- Set up **resource groups** to organize your services.

Step 3: Create an Azure Service

Once you have an Azure subscription:

- Open the **Azure Portal** and go to **"Create a Resource"**.

- Select the **Azure service** you want to use.
- Follow the on-screen instructions to configure the service.

For example, if you choose **Azure SQL Database**, you will:

- Select **SQL Database** from the Azure services list.
- Choose a **server, pricing plan, and database size**.
- Set up **authentication and access permissions**.

Step 4: Connect Azure to Power Apps

After creating your Azure service, you must link it to Power Apps:

- Open **Power Apps Studio**.
- Click on **"Data" > "Add data"**.
- Search for the Azure connector (e.g., **Azure SQL, Azure Blob Storage, or Azure AI**).
- Sign in with your **Azure credentials** and select your resource.
- Once connected, use the data within Power Apps for **forms, galleries, and automation**.

By following these steps, your Power Apps can **access and interact with Azure services**, making them more dynamic and feature-rich.

3. Using Azure Services to Enhance Power Apps

Now that Power Apps is connected to Azure, it's time to explore **how to leverage Azure's capabilities** to enhance app functionality.

1. Storing and Managing Data with Azure SQL Database

Power Apps can store data in various places, but when dealing with **large datasets, complex relationships, or real-time transactions**, Azure SQL Database is the best option.

- **How to Use:**
- Store Power Apps form submissions in **Azure SQL tables**.
- Run **complex queries** to retrieve data efficiently.
- Use **stored procedures** for advanced data processing.
- **Benefits:**
- **Faster performance** compared to SharePoint or Excel.
- **Supports large datasets** without slowing down.
- **Ensures data security and compliance** with enterprise standards.

2. Automating Workflows with Azure Logic Apps

Azure Logic Apps allow Power Apps to **automate tasks, integrate with external services, and manage workflows** without writing complex code.

- **How to Use:**
- Automate notifications when a new record is added.
- Integrate with **Microsoft Teams, Outlook, and third-party services**.
- Schedule **data refreshes** to keep information up-to-date.
- **Benefits:**
- **Reduces manual work** and increases efficiency.
- **Connects Power Apps to other cloud services** easily.
- **Saves time** by handling repetitive processes automatically.

3. Adding AI Capabilities with Azure Cognitive Services

Power Apps can become smarter by integrating **Azure AI and Cognitive Services**. These services enable **speech recognition, image processing, and text analysis**.

- **How to Use:**
- Add a **chatbot** to answer user queries.
- Use **text sentiment analysis** to understand customer feedback.
- Recognize **faces and objects** using AI-powered image processing.
- **Benefits:**
- **Enhances user experience** with intelligent automation.
- **Reduces workload** by automating repetitive decision-making.
- **Improves accuracy** in data analysis and user interactions.

4. Running Custom Code with Azure Functions

Azure Functions allow Power Apps to **execute custom code** whenever specific actions are triggered.

- **How to Use:**
- Run a **custom script** when a button is clicked.
- Perform **real-time calculations** for business applications.
- Automate **data processing tasks** without slowing down Power Apps.
- **Benefits:**
- **Handles complex tasks** without affecting app performance.
- **Scales automatically** based on demand.
- **Reduces development time** by reusing existing functions.

11.2 Integrating Power Apps with Microsoft Teams

Collaboration is the backbone of any successful organization. Whether teams are working remotely or in an office, they need seamless ways to **share information, track progress, and automate tasks**. Power Apps, when integrated with Microsoft Teams, creates a **powerful ecosystem** where businesses can build custom apps that enhance productivity, streamline workflows, and simplify communication—all within a familiar platform.

This integration allows businesses to **create and use apps directly in Teams**, eliminating the need to switch between multiple tools. Whether it's tracking project progress, automating approvals, or managing customer requests, Power Apps and Microsoft Teams work together to make everything **more efficient and organized**.

1. Why Integrate Power Apps with Microsoft Teams?

Microsoft Teams is more than just a chat tool—it serves as a central hub for **communication, collaboration, and automation**. By embedding Power Apps within Teams, businesses can:

- **Enhance productivity:** Employees can access apps directly in Teams without leaving the platform.
- **Automate repetitive tasks:** Reduce manual work by automating workflows.
- **Improve data management:** Store, edit, and retrieve information easily from within Teams.
- **Enhance decision-making:** Provide real-time access to critical business data.

2. *Steps to Integrate Power Apps with Microsoft Teams*

Integrating Power Apps with Microsoft Teams is simple, but to make the most of it, you need to follow a structured approach.

Step 1: Build or Select a Power App

Before adding an app to Teams, you either need to create a new Power App or use an existing one.

- Open **Power Apps Studio** and **create an app** based on your requirements.
- Use **a template** if you need a quick solution or start from scratch for a fully customized experience.
- Ensure the app is designed for collaboration, allowing multiple users to interact with it.

Step 2: Publish the App to Microsoft Teams

Once your app is ready, you need to **publish it inside Teams** so that employees can access it.

- In **Power Apps Studio**, click on **"Settings" > "Add to Teams"**.
- Select the **Teams environment** where the app will be available.
- Click **"Download app"** and follow the setup instructions.

Alternatively, you can share the app via **Power Apps Portal** and send users a direct link.

Step 3: Add the App to a Teams Channel

To make the app accessible within Teams, you need to add it to a **specific channel or team**.

- Open **Microsoft Teams** and go to the **desired team or channel**.
- Click **"+" (Add a Tab)** and select **Power Apps**.

269

- Choose your published app from the list and confirm the setup.

Now, team members can use the app **directly within Teams**, making work **smoother and more efficient**.

Step 4: Automate Workflows with Power Automate

To further enhance the integration, use **Power Automate** to create workflows that **trigger actions based on app interactions**.

- Automate notifications when a new record is added.
- Schedule reports to be shared in Teams automatically.
- Sync app data with other business tools for better tracking.

By integrating Power Apps with Teams, organizations can **simplify processes, reduce workload, and improve collaboration**, making teamwork **more effective and engaging**.

11.3 Building Chatbots with Power Virtual Agents

Customer support, internal help desks, and automated responses are crucial for modern businesses. But hiring support teams for every question can be time-consuming and costly. This is where **Power Virtual Agents** step in—a tool that allows businesses to **create AIpowered chatbots** without requiring any coding knowledge.

Power Virtual Agents enable businesses to **engage with users, answer common questions, and automate repetitive tasks**. These chatbots can be used in **websites, Microsoft Teams, and even Power Apps**, providing **instant assistance** and improving user experiences.

1. Why Use Power Virtual Agents?

- **Instant responses:** Chatbots can handle multiple queries simultaneously, reducing wait times.
- **Automates repetitive tasks:** Frees up employees from answering basic questions.
- **Works across multiple platforms:** Chatbots can be deployed in **Microsoft Teams, websites, and customer portals**.
- **Improves customer satisfaction:** Provides quick, consistent, and accurate responses.

2. Steps to Build a Chatbot with Power Virtual Agents

Creating a chatbot with Power Virtual Agents is straightforward. You don't need advanced programming skills—just a clear understanding of **what your chatbot should do**.

Step 1: Access Power Virtual Agents

To start, go to **Power Virtual Agents Portal** and sign in with your Microsoft account.

- Click **"Create a new bot"**.
- Choose the **language and platform** where the bot will be deployed.
- Name your bot and set up **basic configurations**.

Step 2: Define the Chatbot's Purpose

Think about what the chatbot will be used for. Common use cases include:

- **Customer Support:** Answer FAQs, troubleshoot common problems.

271

- **Employee Assistance:** Provide company policies, IT support, HR inquiries.
- **Sales and Marketing:** Guide customers through product selections.

Once the chatbot's purpose is clear, you can **start building conversations**.

Step 3: Create Chatbot Topics

Topics are predefined conversations that the chatbot can handle.

- Click on **"Topics" > "Create New Topic"**.
- Name the topic (e.g., "Password Reset" or "Order Tracking").
- Define **trigger phrases** (e.g., "How do I reset my password?").
- Add **bot responses** (text, images, or links).
- Use **decision trees** to guide users through different paths.

Step 4: Test and Refine the Chatbot

Once you've added topics, test the chatbot to ensure it responds correctly.

- Use the **built-in chatbot simulator** to check responses.
- Adjust answers if they feel robotic or unclear.
- Improve chatbot flow using **Power Automate** for deeper integration.

Step 5: Deploy the Chatbot

Once everything works smoothly, deploy the chatbot to your chosen platform:

- **In Microsoft Teams:** Publish the bot for internal use.
- **On a Website:** Embed the chatbot in a customer portal.

- **In Power Apps:** Use the chatbot for form submissions or assistance.

By building **AI-powered chatbots**, businesses can provide **quick, 24/7 assistance**, making interactions more **efficient and satisfying** for both employees and customers.

11.4 Leveraging AI and Machine Learning in Power Apps

Technology is evolving at an incredible pace, and businesses are looking for smarter ways to **automate tasks, analyze data, and improve decision-making**. AI and machine learning are no longer futuristic concepts; they are powerful tools that can transform how businesses operate.

Power Apps makes it easy to **integrate AI and machine learning** into everyday applications, helping businesses work more efficiently and provide a better user experience. Whether it's automating data entry, recognizing images, predicting trends, or enhancing customer interactions, AI-driven Power Apps can **streamline processes and improve accuracy**.

1. Why Use AI and Machine Learning in Power Apps?

AI and machine learning allow businesses to **reduce manual effort, speed up operations, and make smarter decisions**. Here's how they make a difference:

- **Automate tedious tasks:** AI can extract information from documents, recognize images, and process data instantly.

- **Improve decision-making:** Machine learning models can predict trends, helping businesses make informed choices.
- **Enhance customer experiences:** AI-powered chatbots and automation tools ensure faster responses and personalized interactions.
- **Increase accuracy:** AI eliminates human errors in data entry and analysis.

2. Steps to Integrate AI in Power Apps

Adding AI to Power Apps is simpler than most people think. Microsoft provides pre-built AI models that can be used without writing complex code.

Step 1: Access AI Builder in Power Apps

To get started, open **Power Apps Studio** and go to **AI Builder**.

- Click on **"Explore"** to see the available AI models.
- Choose a **pre-built AI model** or create a custom one.
- If you're building a custom model, define what it should analyze (text, images, numbers, etc.).

Step 2: Train the AI Model

AI models learn from data, so you need to provide examples.

- Upload sample data for the AI to study (e.g., past customer orders, invoices, or documents).
- Train the model by allowing it to recognize patterns.
- Test the model to ensure it understands and processes data correctly.

Step 3: Integrate the AI Model into Power Apps

Once your AI model is ready, it's time to bring it into Power Apps.

- Open your **Power App** and select the **AI model** from AI Builder.
- Drag and drop the AI component into your app.
- Connect it with a data source (such as a database, SharePoint list, or Excel file).

Now, your app can **automatically recognize text, predict outcomes, or analyze images**, making processes much more efficient.

Step 4: Automate AI Actions with Power Automate

To make the most of AI, combine it with **Power Automate**.

- Set up workflows that trigger AI actions based on user input.
- Automate notifications, data extraction, and report generation.
- Use AI to analyze customer feedback and respond automatically.

By integrating AI into Power Apps, businesses can **save time, reduce errors, and improve efficiency**, all while making smarter decisions.

11.5 Creating Advanced User Interfaces and Experiences

An app is only as good as the experience it provides. Even the most powerful applications can become frustrating if they are **cluttered, confusing, or difficult to navigate**. Creating an **intuitive, visually appealing, and user-friendly** interface is key to ensuring that users get the most out of Power Apps.

A well-designed app should be **easy to use, visually appealing, and highly responsive**. It should guide users seamlessly through tasks, minimizing confusion and improving efficiency.

1. Why Focus on UI and UX in Power Apps?

An advanced user interface (UI) does more than just look good—it enhances how users interact with an app. A well-designed UI and user experience (UX) help:

- **Improve usability:** Users can navigate effortlessly without confusion.
- **Boost efficiency:** A clean layout reduces distractions and speeds up tasks.
- **Enhance engagement:** A visually appealing app encourages users to interact more.
- **Reduce errors:** Clear buttons, labels, and layouts help prevent mistakes.

2. Steps to Build an Advanced UI in Power Apps

Creating a professional-looking and intuitive app requires thoughtful design. Here's how to do it:

Step 1: Use a Consistent Layout

A good app layout ensures that users **find what they need quickly**.

- Stick to a **grid-based design** to keep elements organized.
- Place important buttons and navigation menus in **easily accessible locations**.
- Ensure that text, buttons, and forms are **well-spaced and not cluttered**.

Step 2: Enhance Navigation with Clear Menus and Buttons

Users should be able to **move through the app smoothly**.

- Use **tabs, menus, and icons** for easy navigation.
- Add a **clear home button** that takes users back to the main screen.
- Use **breadcrumb trails** so users always know where they are.

Step 3: Improve Readability with Colors and Fonts

The right color scheme and font choice make a huge difference in usability.

- Stick to **two or three primary colors** to maintain consistency.
- Use **contrasting colors** for buttons and important actions.
- Select **easy-to-read fonts** and ensure text sizes are appropriate.

Step 4: Add Interactive Elements for a Better Experience

An engaging app should **respond to user actions smoothly**.

- Add animations for **smooth transitions** between pages.
- Use **tooltips** to provide extra guidance without cluttering the screen.
- Display **real-time feedback** when users submit forms or make selections.

Step 5: Optimize for Mobile and Different Screen Sizes

Since users access apps from different devices, responsiveness is key.

- Test the app on **mobile, tablet, and desktop** to ensure it works well everywhere.
- Use **flexible layouts** that adjust based on screen size.
- Minimize the number of clicks needed to complete a task.

By focusing on user-friendly design principles, Power Apps can provide an experience that is **intuitive, engaging, and highly efficient**, ensuring users stay productive and satisfied.

Chapter 12: Testing and Debugging Your Apps

Building an app is just the beginning. To ensure that it functions smoothly and provides the best experience for users, thorough **testing and debugging** are essential. No matter how carefully an app is designed, there will always be **errors, inefficiencies, or unexpected issues** that need to be addressed before deployment.

Testing helps identify these problems, ensuring that the app is **reliable, efficient, and free from critical bugs**. Debugging, on the other hand, is the process of finding and fixing errors so the app runs as expected. A well-tested app is **faster, more stable, and delivers a better user experience**.

12.1 The Importance of Testing Power Apps

Testing is not just about checking if an app works—it's about making sure it works **well**. A single overlooked issue can frustrate users, disrupt workflows, or even cause data loss. That's why thorough testing is a necessary step before launching any Power App.

Why Is Testing Important?

- **Ensures Reliability:** A properly tested app will function consistently under different conditions.
- **Improves Performance:** Identifying bottlenecks and fixing slow responses can improve app speed.
- **Prevents Errors:** Catching issues early reduces the risk of failures when the app is live.
- **Enhances User Experience:** A smooth, bug-free app keeps users engaged and satisfied.
- **Saves Time and Cost:** Fixing issues before deployment prevents costly problems later.

Types of Testing in Power Apps

Testing should be **thorough and well-planned** to cover different aspects of the app. Here are some key testing methods:

1. **Functional Testing:** Ensures that every feature works as expected.
2. **Performance Testing:** Measures how fast the app loads and responds under different conditions.
3. **Usability Testing:** Evaluates how easy it is for users to navigate and complete tasks.

4. **Security Testing:** Checks for vulnerabilities to protect sensitive data.

5. **Integration Testing:** Ensures smooth interaction between Power Apps and other connected services.

Skipping testing or rushing through it can lead to serious issues later. A structured approach ensures that the app runs **smoothly and efficiently**, avoiding unnecessary frustration for users.

12.2 How to Use the App Checker Tool

Testing a Power App doesn't have to be complicated. Microsoft provides built-in tools to help developers **identify and fix errors quickly**. One of the most useful tools is the **App Checker**, which scans the app for issues and provides recommendations for improvement.

What is the App Checker Tool?

The App Checker is a built-in feature in Power Apps that helps **detect and resolve issues** before deployment. It checks the app for:

- **Formula errors** that might cause incorrect calculations or broken functions.
- **Performance issues** that can slow down the app.
- **Accessibility problems** to ensure a smooth experience for all users.
- **Security risks** that could expose sensitive data.

Using the App Checker regularly helps ensure that the app is **opti-**

mized, efficient, and user-friendly.

Step-by-Step Guide to Using the App Checker

Step 1: Open the App Checker

- Launch **Power Apps Studio** and open the app you want to test.
- Click on the **"App Checker"** icon in the top-right corner of the screen.

Step 2: Review the Detected Issues

Once the App Checker runs a scan, it categorizes issues into different sections:

- **Errors:** Critical problems that must be fixed before the app can function properly.
- **Warnings:** Issues that may affect performance but won't stop the app from running.
- **Accessibility Issues:** Improvements needed to make the app more user-friendly.

Step 3: Fix Formula and Logic Errors

- If there are formula errors, click on the issue to view **the problematic formula**.
- Edit the formula directly to correct the syntax or logic.
- Use **error messages and tooltips** to understand the problem.

Step 4: Improve Performance Issues

- The App Checker highlights areas where the app **loads slowly or**

uses too many resources.

- Reduce unnecessary data calls and use **delegation techniques** to handle large datasets efficiently.
- Optimize image sizes and remove unused components to improve app speed.

Step 5: Address Accessibility Problems

- The tool provides **recommendations for improving accessibility**, such as adjusting color contrast or adding screen reader support.
- Make necessary changes to ensure **users with disabilities can navigate the app easily**.

Step 6: Re-run the App Checker

- After making fixes, **run the App Checker again** to confirm that all issues are resolved.
- Continue testing until no critical issues remain.

12.3 Debugging Common Errors and Issues

Debugging is the process of finding and fixing **unexpected issues** in an app. Some errors might stop the app from functioning, while others may cause **slow performance, incorrect results, or missing data**. The key to effective debugging is understanding the root cause of the problem and applying the right solution.

Common Errors in Power Apps and How to Fix Them

1. Formula and Syntax Errors

- These occur when there's a mistake in an expression or a formula.
- If Power Apps highlights an error in red, it means the formula is incorrect.

Solution:

- Check for **misspelled functions** or missing parentheses.
- Ensure that all variables and data sources exist and are referenced correctly.
- Use **the formula bar's error messages** to understand the issue.

2. Data Connection Failures

- Apps often rely on external data sources like SharePoint, SQL, or Excel. If the app fails to fetch or update data, users will see errors.

Solution:

- Check the **data connection settings** and refresh them if necessary.
- Ensure that the correct permissions are granted to access the data.
- If using APIs, verify that the API key or authentication method is correct.

3. Slow Performance Issues

- Apps that take too long to load or respond poorly can frustrate users.

- Large data sets, unoptimised queries, and unnecessary controls can cause lag.

Solution:

- **Use delegation** when working with large data sources to improve performance.
- Reduce unnecessary formulas and optimize screen transitions.
- Compress images and remove unused elements.

4. Screen Freezing or Crashes

- If an app crashes frequently, it may be due to **memory overload or faulty scripts**.

Solution:

- Reduce the number of concurrent data calls.
- Optimize screen navigation by removing unnecessary transitions.
- Test the app on different devices to identify the cause.

5. Missing or Incorrect Data Display

- Users may experience issues where fields show **blank values or incorrect information**.

Solution:

- Ensure that the correct **data types** are used.
- Check if filters and conditions are applied correctly.

- Verify that there are no restrictions on data access.

Effective debugging ensures that the app runs **smoothly and without errors**, creating a **seamless experience for users**.

12.4 Testing Apps on Multiple Devices and Platforms

People use different devices to access apps—**smartphones, tablets, desktops, and even web browsers**. Each platform may display the app differently, and without proper testing, users might experience **broken layouts, slow performance, or compatibility issues**.

Why Cross-Device Testing Is Important

- Ensures that the app works on both **Android and iOS** devices.
- Confirms that buttons, images, and layouts adjust properly across **different screen sizes**.
- Detects performance issues on **low-power devices** that might not handle heavy processing well.
- Prevents **platform-specific bugs** that could cause errors on one device but not another.

How to Test Power Apps on Different Devices

Step 1: Test in Power Apps Studio

- Use **Preview Mode** in Power Apps Studio to check the app's **layout and functionality**.
- Click on different buttons, enter data, and navigate between screens to ensure everything works smoothly.

Step 2: Use the Power Apps Mobile App

- Download the **Power Apps Mobile App** on both Android and iOS.
- Open the app on a phone and tablet to check if the **interface adjusts correctly**.
- Test for **touch responsiveness**, scrolling issues, and slow-loading screens.

Step 3: Test in Web Browsers

- Open the app on different browsers like **Chrome, Edge, Safari, and Firefox**.
- Check if all functions work **without layout issues or missing features**.

Step 4: Simulate Low-Speed Networks

- Some users may access the app on a **slow internet connection**.
- Use browser developer tools to simulate **2G or 3G speeds** and test how the app performs.
- Optimize images and data calls to improve speed.

Step 5: Gather User Feedback

- Ask a small group of users to test the app on their devices.
- Collect feedback about **performance, layout, and any issues** they experience.
- Make necessary adjustments before full deployment.

Testing on multiple devices prevents **unexpected problems** and ensures that the app provides a **consistent experience for all users**.

12.5 Version Control and App Rollback

Apps constantly evolve as **new features are added, bugs are fixed, and improvements are made**. However, sometimes an update may cause **unexpected issues**, making it necessary to **revert to a previous version**. Version control ensures that each update is **properly tracked**, allowing developers to restore older versions when needed.

Why Version Control is Important

- Allows you to **restore an earlier version** if a new update breaks the app.
- Helps track **who made changes and when**.
- Enables testing new features without affecting the live app.

How to Manage Version Control in Power Apps

Step 1: Enable Versioning in Power Apps

- Power Apps automatically saves versions every time you make changes.
- To view previous versions, go to **File > Save & Publish > See All Versions**.

Step 2: Save a Stable Version Before Major Changes

- Before making big changes, save a **backup version** so you can return to it if needed.

288

- Use **meaningful version names** like "Stable_v1" or "New_UI_Test."

Step 3: Roll Back to a Previous Version

- If an update causes problems, open **Version History** and select an earlier version.
- Click **Restore**, and Power Apps will revert to the selected version.

Step 4: Test Before Publishing

- Before releasing a new version, test it thoroughly to avoid **breaking existing functionality**.
- Use a **test environment** to try out changes before applying them to the live app.

Step 5: Communicate Changes with Users

- If rolling back to a previous version, inform users about **why the change was necessary**.
- Keep a record of past issues and solutions to **prevent repeating the same mistakes**.

By managing versions carefully, developers can **experiment with new features** without risking the stability of the app. Rollback options ensure that if something goes wrong, there's always a way to **restore a working version quickly**.

Chapter 13: Publishing, Sharing, and Distributing Power Apps

After building and testing an app, the next step is to **publish and share it** so others can start using it. A well-designed app serves no purpose if it remains locked in development. It needs to reach the right users—whether they are employees in an organization, customers, or team members—so it can deliver value and improve efficiency.

Publishing ensures that the latest version of the app is **available and functional**, while sharing allows users to **access and interact** with it. Whether you are rolling out an app for a small team or an entire company, following the right process ensures a **smooth deployment**.

13.1 How to Publish Your Power Apps

Publishing an app means making the final version **available for users**. It allows people to access the app with the latest updates and ensures that any modifications made during development are properly saved.

Steps to Publish a Power App

Step 1: Open the App in Power Apps Studio

- Launch **Power Apps Studio** and open the app that you want to publish.
- Review the app's layout, functionality, and settings to ensure everything is correct.

Step 2: Save the Latest Version

- Click on **File > Save** to ensure that all changes are stored.
- Saving the latest version prevents any **loss of progress** or missing updates.

Step 3: Test the App Before Publishing

- Before making the app live, test its features by running it in **Preview Mode**.
- Click through each screen, enter sample data, and verify that buttons, forms, and navigation work as expected.

Step 4: Publish the App

- Go to **File > Save & Publish** and select **Publish This Version**.
- This action makes the latest version **available to users**, replacing the previous one.

Step 5: Confirm the Update

- Once published, a confirmation message will appear.

- If needed, you can **revert to an earlier version** by accessing the version history.

Publishing keeps your app up to date, ensuring that users always access the latest features and improvements.

13.2 Sharing Apps with Users and Teams

Once the app is published, it needs to be shared with the right people. Power Apps provides different ways to **control access** and ensure that only authorized users can interact with the app.

Who Can You Share the App With?

- **Individual Users** – Specific people who need access to the app.
- **Teams or Departments** – Groups working on shared projects.
- **Entire Organization** – Everyone in the company, if the app is intended for company-wide use.

Steps to Share a Power App

Step 1: Open the App Settings

- In **Power Apps Studio**, go to **File > Share**.
- A list of sharing options will appear.

Step 2: Add Users or Groups

- Enter the **email addresses** of individuals or groups you want to share the app with.

- You can also select **Azure Active Directory groups** for companywide sharing.

Step 3: Set Permissions

- Decide what level of access each user should have:
- **User Access** – Allows people to use the app but not modify it.
- **Co-Owner Access** – Grants permission to edit and update the app.
- For most cases, users should only have **basic access** to prevent unintended changes.

Step 4: Send the Invitation

- Click **Share**, and the users will receive an **email notification** with a link to access the app.
- They can open it using **Power Apps Mobile App** or a web browser.

Step 5: Monitor and Manage Access

- At any time, you can **remove users, change permissions, or add new members**.
- If an app is no longer needed, you can disable access or archive it.

Best Practices for Sharing Power Apps

- **Ensure data security** by limiting access to only necessary users.
- **Test the app before sharing** to avoid distributing an incomplete or faulty version.
- **Provide clear instructions** so users understand how to navigate

and use the app effectively.

Sharing makes it possible for teams to **collaborate, automate tasks, and streamline workflows** efficiently. A well-shared app ensures that the right people have access, **enhancing productivity and user engagement**.

13.3 Managing App Permissions and Access

Controlling access to an app is crucial to ensure the right people can use or modify it. Power Apps provides flexible permission settings, allowing developers to **define roles** for each user.

Types of Permissions in Power Apps

- **Owner** – Has full control over the app, including the ability to edit, share, and delete it.
- **Co-owner** – Can modify the app but cannot delete or transfer ownership.
- **User** – Can access and use the app but cannot make any changes.

Steps to Manage Permissions

Step 1: Open the Sharing Settings

- In **Power Apps Studio**, select the app you want to manage.
- Click on **File > Share** to open the permissions menu.

Step 2: Add Users or Groups

- Enter the **email addresses** of individuals or groups who need access.
- If the app is meant for a department or the entire company, use **Azure Active Directory Groups**.

Step 3: Assign Permission Levels

- Select the appropriate role for each user:
- **Co-owners** can assist in modifying the app.
- **Users** can only interact with it.
- Avoid granting unnecessary editing rights to prevent unintended changes.

Step 4: Save and Confirm

- Click **Share**, and Power Apps will send an **invitation link** to the users.
- Users can now **access the app** based on their assigned permissions.

Best Practices for Managing Permissions

- **Limit co-owner roles** to a few trusted individuals.
- **Review permissions regularly** to ensure no unauthorized access.
- **Use security groups** instead of adding users one by one for easier management.

By managing permissions carefully, you **protect data, maintain control, and create a structured user experience**.

13.4 Creating and Managing App Environments

An environment in Power Apps is a **workspace** where apps, data, and user roles are organized. Properly managing environments allows businesses to **separate development, testing, and production** to ensure smooth app deployment.

Why Are Environments Important?

- Keep **testing and live apps separate** to avoid disruptions.
- Control **who can develop and modify** apps within a workspace.
- Improve **security and data management** across different teams.

Types of Environments

1. **Default Environment** – Automatically created for every organization and used for basic app development.
2. **Production Environment** – Designed for live apps with strict access controls.
3. **Sandbox Environment** – Used for testing new features without affecting the live version.
4. **Developer Environment** – Created for personal testing and development.

Steps to Create and Manage an Environment

Step 1: Access the Power Platform Admin Center

- Open the **Power Platform Admin Center** and navigate to **Environments**.

Step 2: Create a New Environment

- Click **New Environment** and give it a clear name (e.g., "Testing Workspace").
- Choose the **region** and the **type of environment** (Production, Sandbox, etc.).

Step 3: Assign Security Roles

- Define **who can access and manage** the environment.
- Assign roles such as **Environment Admins** (who control settings) and **Makers** (who can build apps).

Step 4: Connect to a Database (Optional)

- If needed, link the environment to **Dataverse** to store and manage data.

Step 5: Save and Monitor Usage

- Once the environment is set up, **track performance, security, and user activity**.

Best Practices for Managing Environments

- **Use separate environments** for development and production to avoid issues.
- **Restrict access** to prevent unnecessary modifications.
- **Monitor resource usage** to avoid performance slowdowns.

By structuring environments properly, organizations can **develop**

and deploy apps efficiently while maintaining security and performance.

13.5 Distributing Apps in the Organization

Once an app is ready, it must be **delivered to the right users** in a way that ensures smooth adoption and usage. A well-planned distribution process helps teams **quickly access the app and integrate it into their workflows**.

Ways to Distribute Power Apps

- **Direct Sharing** – Send access links to specific users.
- **Power Apps Mobile App** – Allow users to download and run apps on their phones.
- **Microsoft Teams Integration** – Embed the app inside Teams for easy collaboration.
- **Company App Store** – If the organization has an internal portal, publish the app there.

Steps to Distribute an App

Step 1: Choose the Distribution Method

- If the app is for a **specific team**, sharing via email or Teams is ideal.
- For **company-wide distribution**, use Power Apps portals or an internal app store.

Step 2: Ensure Users Have the Right Access

- Double-check **permissions and security settings** before rolling out the app.
- Set up **single sign-on (SSO)** to simplify user authentication.

Step 3: Provide Training and Support

- Send out **user guides** or offer a short demo to help users get started.
- Create a **support channel** where users can ask questions.

Step 4: Monitor Adoption and Gather Feedback

- Use **Power Apps analytics** to track usage and identify areas for improvement.
- Ask for feedback and roll out updates based on user needs.

Best Practices for Distributing Apps

- **Keep the launch simple**—avoid complex rollout processes.
- **Provide easy access** through company-approved platforms.
- **Encourage feedback** to enhance the app over time.

By focusing on proper distribution, organizations **ensure that apps are widely adopted, easy to access, and useful for employees**.

Chapter 14: Power Apps in Business Applications

Technology is transforming the way businesses operate, making tasks faster, smarter, and more efficient. Power Apps plays a vital role in this transformation, **helping businesses streamline their sales, marketing, and customer service processes**. With its ability to create customized applications without requiring advanced coding skills, Power Apps allows companies to develop solutions that perfectly fit their needs.

From managing sales pipelines to enhancing customer interactions, Power Apps provides businesses with the tools to work **smarter, not harder**. By using automated workflows, data-driven insights, and user-friendly apps, teams can focus on what truly matters—building strong relationships with customers and driving growth.

14.1 Power Apps for Sales, Marketing, and Customer Service

Sales, marketing, and customer service are the backbone of any business. These areas require **constant communication, organized workflows, and real-time data** to ensure efficiency and customer satisfaction. Power Apps helps businesses in these sectors by providing tailored solutions that improve team productivity and enhance customer engagement.

Power Apps for Sales

Sales teams rely on **data, automation, and quick decision-making** to close deals successfully. Power Apps makes this process smoother by providing sales representatives with real-time insights and easy to use tools for managing leads and customer interactions.

How Power Apps Can Help the Sales Team

- **Lead Management** – Track and update customer leads in a centralized app.
- **Sales Pipeline Tracking** – Monitor deal progress and identify potential bottlenecks.
- **Mobile Access** – Allow sales representatives to update customer details from anywhere.
- **Automated Follow-Ups** – Set reminders for customer interactions to avoid missed opportunities.

Steps to Create a Sales Management App in Power Apps

Step 1: Define the Purpose of the App

Before building the app, list the key sales processes you want to manage. For example, tracking leads, managing appointments, or storing customer details.

Step 2: Choose a Data Source

Select where the app will store customer and sales data. Power Apps integrates with **Microsoft Dataverse, SharePoint, and Excel**, making it easy to pull in existing data.

Step 3: Design the User Interface

- Use the drag-and-drop editor to create a simple and clean layout.
- Add text fields for customer names, contact details, and deal status.
- Include buttons for updating lead progress and setting reminders.

Step 4: Add Automation

- Set up automated notifications to alert the sales team when a deal is about to close.
- Use Power Automate to send follow-up emails or schedule meetings directly from the app.

Step 5: Test and Deploy the App

- Ensure the app functions correctly by testing different scenarios.
- Share the app with the sales team and train them on how to use it effectively.

By implementing Power Apps, sales teams **spend less time on manual data entry and more time closing deals**.

Power Apps for Marketing

Marketing teams handle **campaigns, customer engagement, and brand awareness**, all of which require detailed planning and execution. With Power Apps, marketers can manage their projects more effectively by using custom apps to **track campaign performance, automate repetitive tasks, and improve audience targeting**.

How Power Apps Can Enhance Marketing Efforts

- **Campaign Management** – Keep track of multiple marketing campaigns in one place.
- **Customer Segmentation** – Organize leads based on demographics, interests, or behavior.
- **Content Approval Workflows** – Streamline the process of getting marketing materials approved.
- **Event Management** – Track event registrations and send automatic reminders to attendees.

Steps to Create a Marketing Campaign Management App

Step 1: Identify the Key Features

Determine what the app should do—whether it's tracking campaign progress, storing customer responses, or managing advertising budgets.

Step 2: Connect to a Marketing Database

Link the app to sources like **Excel, Dataverse, or a CRM system** to pull in campaign and customer data.

Step 3: Design an Interactive Dashboard

- Create a dashboard that displays campaign performance metrics

in real-time.
- Add charts and graphs to visualize audience engagement.

Step 4: Automate Notifications and Approvals

- Use Power Automate to send notifications when campaigns reach key milestones.
- Set up approval workflows for marketing materials before they go live.

Step 5: Share the App with the Marketing Team

- Ensure all team members have the right access and can collaborate seamlessly.

With Power Apps, marketing teams **gain better control over campaigns and improve their ability to engage with customers effectively**.

Power Apps for Customer Service

Providing excellent customer service is essential for any business. Customers expect **quick responses, personalized support, and a seamless experience**. Power Apps enables businesses to **build custom solutions that enhance service quality, track customer interactions, and automate routine support tasks**.

How Power Apps Can Improve Customer Service

- **Centralized Customer Support Portal** – Keep all customer queries, complaints, and resolutions in one place.
- **Automated Ticketing System** – Assign tickets to support agents based on priority.
- **Chatbot Integration** – Provide instant answers to common questions.
- **Feedback Collection** – Gather customer opinions to improve service quality.

Steps to Build a Customer Support App

Step 1: Define the Features

Decide what the app should include, such as a ticketing system, a FAQ section, or live chat support.

Step 2: Connect to a Customer Database

Use Power Apps to integrate with existing **CRM systems, Excel, or Microsoft Dataverse**.

Step 3: Create a User-Friendly Interface

- Add a form where customers can submit their issues.
- Include a dashboard for support agents to track open tickets.

Step 4: Set Up Automated Responses

- Use Power Automate to send confirmation emails when customers submit requests.
- Assign high-priority tickets to agents immediately.

Step 5: Monitor Performance and Improve

- Collect data on response times and customer satisfaction.
- Make updates based on user feedback to enhance the support experience.

By using Power Apps, businesses can **resolve customer issues faster, improve satisfaction, and build long-term loyalty**.

14.2 Automating HR Processes with Power Apps

Human Resources is the backbone of any organization, responsible for hiring, training, payroll, employee records, and performance evaluations. Managing these tasks manually can be overwhelming, leading to delays, errors, and frustration. Power Apps provides HR teams with **custom-built solutions to automate processes, streamline communication, and improve employee experience**.

How Power Apps Can Improve HR Efficiency

- **Automated Employee Onboarding** – Simplifies the hiring process by guiding new employees through necessary steps.
- **Leave and Attendance Tracking** – Keeps records of absences, approvals, and schedules.
- **Performance Management** – Stores performance reviews, feedback, and goal tracking in a centralized system.
- **Payroll Management** – Ensures accuracy in salary processing and tax deductions.

Steps to Automate HR Tasks with Power Apps

Step 1: Identify Key HR Tasks to Automate

List out processes that are time-consuming or prone to errors, such as onboarding, leave requests, or payroll management.

Step 2: Choose a Data Source

Power Apps integrates with **Excel, SharePoint, Dataverse, and HR management software** to store and retrieve employee data.

Step 3: Design a User-Friendly Interface

- Create digital forms for employees to submit leave requests or update their personal information.
- Develop a dashboard for HR managers to view pending approvals and track employee performance.

Step 4: Automate Approvals and Notifications

- Use Power Automate to send automatic alerts when a new employee completes onboarding steps.
- Set up approval workflows for leave requests to notify managers instantly.

Step 5: Test and Deploy the App

- Run trial tests with HR staff and employees.
- Gather feedback to refine features and improve usability.

By leveraging Power Apps, HR teams can **reduce paperwork, improve accuracy, and focus on building a positive workplace culture**.

14.3 Streamlining Operations and Inventory Management

Managing operations and inventory efficiently is crucial for any business. Keeping track of **stock levels, supply chain movements, and equipment usage** can be challenging, especially when done manually. Power Apps simplifies inventory and operations management by providing businesses with **custom apps that track, analyze, and automate essential tasks**.

How Power Apps Enhances Inventory and Operations

- **Real-Time Stock Monitoring** – Keeps inventory records updated automatically.
- **Order and Supplier Management** – Tracks orders, deliveries, and supplier details.
- **Barcode Scanning Integration** – Speeds up stocktaking and item tracking.
- **Automated Restocking Alerts** – Notifies teams when stock levels drop below a set limit.

Steps to Build an Inventory Management App

Step 1: Define Your Business Needs

Determine what you need to track—product stock, raw materials, shipping details, or supplier contacts.

Step 2: Select a Data Source

Choose where inventory records will be stored, such as **Dataverse, Excel, or SharePoint**.

Step 3: Build the Inventory Dashboard

309

- Include fields for item names, quantities, purchase dates, and supplier details.
- Use dropdown menus to categorize products and make searching easier.

Step 4: Add Automation for Stock Alerts

- Set up Power Automate to send notifications when inventory is low.
- Create an automatic ordering system that triggers purchase requests when stock reaches a certain level.

Step 5: Enable Barcode Scanning for Quick Updates

Power Apps allows integration with barcode scanning, making stock management **faster and more accurate**. Employees can scan product labels to update inventory records instantly.

Step 6: Deploy and Train Staff

- Test the app with a small group before rolling it out companywide.
- Train employees on how to use the system to prevent errors.

By using Power Apps for inventory management, businesses **reduce manual errors, optimize stock levels, and improve overall efficiency in operations**.

14.4 Power Apps in Finance and Accounting

Finance and accounting teams handle **critical business operations**, including budgeting, expenses, financial reporting, and compliance. Accuracy and efficiency in these areas are essential for the company's financial health. Power Apps helps finance teams **eliminate manual paperwork, automate calculations, and ensure real-time access to financial data**.

How Power Apps Supports Finance and Accounting

- **Expense Tracking** – Employees can submit expenses with receipts, and managers can approve them digitally.
- **Invoice Processing** – Automates billing and payment tracking to avoid delays.
- **Budget Management** – Provides real-time visibility into financial performance.
- **Compliance Monitoring** – Ensures all financial transactions follow regulations.

Steps to Create a Finance and Accounting App

Step 1: Identify the Key Finance Tasks to Automate
Determine what processes require the most time—expense approvals, invoice tracking, or financial forecasting.

Step 2: Choose a Secure Data Source
Finance data must be stored securely in **Dataverse, SQL databases, or SharePoint** to ensure compliance.

Step 3: Build an Expense and Invoice Management System

- Employees can upload receipts and request reimbursements.

- Managers can review and approve expenses through the app.
- Automate invoice tracking to send alerts for unpaid bills.

Step 4: Integrate with Existing Accounting Software

Power Apps works seamlessly with **Microsoft Dynamics 365, QuickBooks, and other finance platforms** to sync data.

Step 5: Automate Financial Reports

- Use Power Automate to generate monthly financial summaries.
- Set up dashboards that display revenue, expenses, and profit margins in real time.

Step 6: Ensure Data Security and Compliance

Financial data must be protected. Use role-based access control to **limit who can view and edit financial records**.

By adopting Power Apps, finance teams **gain better control over expenses, reduce human errors, and improve decision-making with real-time financial insights**.

Power Apps is revolutionizing business operations by simplifying complex tasks and empowering teams with efficient digital solutions. Whether it's HR teams automating employee management, inventory managers tracking stock with real-time data, or finance departments ensuring accurate expense reporting, Power Apps helps organizations save time, reduce errors, and enhance productivity.

Conclusion

Technology is no longer a luxury—it is a necessity that determines the success and efficiency of every business. As organizations strive to keep up with evolving market demands, the ability to **automate processes, simplify workflows, and enhance productivity** has become more crucial than ever. Power Apps is not just a tool; it is a **game-changer** that gives businesses the power to **create custom solutions without the need for extensive technical expertise**.

Throughout this book, we have explored how Power Apps transforms different aspects of business operations, from **human resources and finance to inventory management and customer service**. Each chapter has shown how **automation and digital innovation** can replace outdated manual tasks, minimize errors, and provide businesses with **real-time insights** that drive smarter decision-making.

The Power of Transformation

Adopting Power Apps is more than just **implementing new technology**—it is about **changing the way businesses operate, think, and grow**. It enables organizations to:

- **Empower Employees** – By automating tedious tasks, employees can focus on meaningful work that contributes to business success.
- **Improve Accuracy and Efficiency** – Manual errors in finance, HR, and operations are significantly reduced, leading to **greater precision and reliability**.
- **Enhance Collaboration** – Teams can work together seamlessly, accessing shared data and insights from a centralized platform.
- **Boost Customer Experience** – By streamlining service processes, businesses can respond **faster, more effectively, and with greater personalization**.

A Future of Endless Possibilities

The true beauty of Power Apps is its **endless adaptability**. No matter the size or industry of a business, there is always **an opportunity to innovate, refine, and improve**. Whether an organization needs **better inventory tracking, seamless expense management, or automated HR workflows**, Power Apps provides a solution tailored to those needs.

More importantly, Power Apps is not a **one-time implementation**—it is a **continuous journey**. As businesses grow, so do their challenges and demands. But with Power Apps, companies are never left behind. They can **evolve, expand, and create new applications** to meet changing business needs, ensuring they stay ahead of the

competition.

The ability to innovate is what separates successful businesses from struggling ones. Power Apps offers every organization the **freedom to design, build, and implement solutions** that cater to their specific needs, without the barriers of traditional software development. It puts **control in the hands of businesses**, allowing them to be proactive rather than reactive in a fast-moving world.

For those who embrace Power Apps, the possibilities are limitless. With the right vision and commitment, businesses can **transform their processes, maximize efficiency, and create a future driven by innovation and success**.

Thank You!!

Made in United States
Troutdale, OR
04/10/2025

30506892R00186